To michael
with best wishes
a long and healthy
Harold Kalnick

TREE OF LIFE

TREE OF LIFE

An Anthology of Articles Appearing in *The Jewish Vegetarian*, 1966-1974

Edited by
Philip L. Pick

SOUTH BRUNSWICK AND NEW YORK: A. S. BARNES AND COMPANY
LONDON: THOMAS YOSELOFF LTD

A. S. Barnes and Co., Inc.
Cranbury, New Jersey 08512

Thomas Yoseloff Ltd
Magdalen House
136-148 Tooley Street
London SE1 2TT, England

For additional information contact
The Jewish Vegetarian Society
International Headquarters
Bet Teva
855 Finchley Road
London NW11 8LX, England

Library of Congress Cataloging in Publication Data

Main entry under title:

Tree of life.

Includes bibliographical references.
1. Vegetarianism — Addresses, essays, lectures.
I. Pick, Philip L.   II. Jewish vegetarian.
TX392.T73   1977   296.7'4   76-18476
ISBN 0-498-01945-4

PRINTED IN THE UNITED STATES OF AMERICA

Contents

5

Foreword

An anthology is an instrument for picking out and preserving the best and most lasting contributions that have appeared in a journal or in a series of books, pointing the way to their particular purpose. One does not dare draw parallels with the Bible—L'Havdil !—but the principle is there. The canonisation of some Books and the exclusion of others came about, says the *Jewish Encyclopedia*, because the national literature had progressed enough to possess a large number of works from which a selection might be made.

The Greek Anthology was compiled ·as a collection of ancient Hellenic poetry extending from about 70 B.C. to A.D. 1000, a period of almost seventeen centuries. The word *anthology* is Greek and derives from flowers, means a gathering of flowers, a garland, the choice, the best, chef d'oeuvre, masterpiece.

This anthology aims at nothing so exalted. For its purpose the secondary meaning of anthology is more appropriate; a compendium, an epitome, a multum in parvo, all that has been said in large reproduced in small.

I can claim for myself a certain acknowledged place as an anthologist extending over forty years, from my *Yisroel* in 1932, through my *Golden Peacock* in 1952, and my *The Way We Think* in 1970. So when Philip Leon Pick, the president of the Jewish Vegetarian Society, told me of his intention to compile an anthology, a selection from past issues of *The Jewish Vegetarian*, which he edits, and asked me to write a foreword, I was happy to comply. It is in a way singing for my supper—doing something for the Society in return for the honour it did me by electing me a patron.

So here it is! The anthology ranges from the expositions of several master Jewish writers telling us why they are vegetarians—Agnon, Israel's Nobel Prize winner for literature ("as devout a vegetarian as he is a Jew"), and Melech Ravitch—to great Jewish religious leaders like Israeli Chief Rabbi Kook and the Kamenister Maggid expounding the religious basis for vegetarianism, ("Let the commandment 'Thou Shalt Not Kill' be understood to include all living creatures") and other rabbis—Rabbi Joseph Rosenfeld, Rabbi Ben-Shemer, Rabbi Everett Gendler and the Revd S. Clayman—pursuing the same thought.

There are selections from the editor's discourses in each issue of the journal, among them "Is it Kosher?" and "The Festival of Freedom."

Did you know that among the many famous vegetarians is comedian Marty Feldman, an honorary member of the Jewish Vegetarian Society? He reminds me of Sholem Aleichem's dictum, "Laugh! Laughing is Health! Laughing is Good for You!"

Did you know that there are vegetarian centenarians, one in Bournemouth who at 105 still works every day?

And that many Barmitzvah boys, some of the second generation, insist on their Barmitzvah parties being all vegetarian?

Did you know that there are about 80,000 vegetarians in Israel—nearly four percent of the population? I am delighted to commend this anthology on vegetarian thought.

Joseph Leftwich

Acknowledgments

Our grateful thanks to
Eric Lockwood Cummings
of Windermere, England,
for his generous help,
without which this
publication would not
have seen the light of day.

FOR A VEGETARIAN WORLD

Introduction

The many requests for articles which have appeared in *The Jewish Vegetarian*, and the fact that the issues concerned were often no longer available, indicated a need for a volume such as this.

Some of these enquiries have come from remote spots such as Kenya, Alaska, Guiana, and even a village somewhere in the Republic of China. They are usually couched in laboriously written English with profound expressions of deep fraternal friendship and multitudinous thanks in advance. In such cases it must be most disheartening for the writer to receive a negative reply.

This experience proves the power of the written word and the geographical penetration it can achieve; it also reminds one that this impact is limited to the length of time that elapses before the matter is finally consigned to the wastepaper collection.

The strength and weakness in propagating ideas through print rest on the ephemeral nature of the periodical or paper concerned. After all, an important supplementary use for newspapers is for wrapping sundry goods, while monthlies and quarterlies have proved most useful in leveling up the odd table leg. *The Jewish Vegetarian*, however, does not seem to fulfil these secondary functions at all well; most of them are eventually bound in sets or sent to acquaintances with the admirable object of undermining their carnivorous propensities.

This is just one of the reasons why this little book has been bound; that it might find a permanent corner in the bookcase, to be taken out and read at random in the odd moment. Occasionally it might give some pleasure (perhaps a glimmer of inspiration) to a visitor; sometimes it may be loaned to a friend and introduce a new way of life. Sometimes it may even be returned to its owner! It is certain, however, that its "shelf life" will be longer than that of any periodical.

In these days of unattached thinking, some constructive philosophy in life has become an overriding necessity. Accordingly, the articles have been selected with the object of generating thought on a subject which offers the only known antidote to the present world malaise. We are often shocked at other people's habits but cannot see our own in the right perspective. Aborigines digging at the root of a tree for maggots to provide their daily food while ignoring the fruit the tree produces, are no worse than the sophisticated eaters of escargots, scampi, or lambs' tongues. In both cases it is the divine process of thought that is absent.

Most books written on vegetarianism deal with facts—facts of vegetarian life, economics, nutrition, environment, cruelty, and health, but with one or two exceptions books on vegetarian thought or opinion are very few and far between and are usually limited to pamphlet proportions. This book, therefore, comprises all opinion and little or no facts, and I hope that some of the thoughts expressed will, somewhere and at some time, strike a chord in the reader's heart or mind, and help his or her resolve toward the attainment of a happier, healthier, and fuller way of life.

To convey birthday greetings, for an occasion such as Chanucah or Christmas, sent anonymously to someone who might benefit thereby, or just to show one's sincere feelings to a dear friend—the gift of this little volume will satisfy the giver, and I am sure, be appreciated by the recipient.

Of even greater importance, a contribution will have been made, however minute, toward that golden age "when they shall no longer hurt nor destroy."

TREE OF LIFE

Why I Am A Vegetarian

The subject matter of this article could be dealt with in seven words—"Because my parents were vegetarian before me." I cannot therefore claim credit as many others can, for making a personal decision either through sheer common sense or through compassion for my fellow creatures. I simply had no option, it was my parents who had made the decision. I therefore think it best to narrate how *they* came to this way of life and why I am grateful for the boon I inherited.

My mother was born in the East End of London in 1882. In those days the ports were open and refugees escaping from the murderous Russian pogroms streamed into London docks causing unbelievable overcrowding and misery. My mother was the eldest of six children; her father had died at the age of 35, traveling steerage from Poland to London. He could not decide where it was best for his family to starve. Tuberculosis was rife and the Missionary Societies offered the only hope. However, apart from the Salvation Army, they demanded formal change of religion before handing over a blanket and two loaves of bread. It is a saga of courage and resolution that these wretched people, trapped on all sides, invariably accepted the alternative of starvation sooner than forsake the faith of their fathers. In due course relief organizations set up a soup kitchen and each person in the long queue received a daily bowl of soup.

It was customary in those days, for those who could afford the luxury, to have a chicken running around the living room until the time arrived for it to be served up at the table. Once when only a child, my mother became very attached to such a chicken, and in due course she was instructed to take it to the "shochet" and to bring back its lifeless body for subsequent mealtimes. Under pressure, she took the bird on its last journey, but whilst waiting for its throat to be cut she went into hysterics and dashed home, crying all the way. This crying continued on and off for weeks. She had lost a dear little friend.

At times, along with thousands of others, her mother would take her to hear that great and saintly preacher, the Reverend T. Maccoby (the Kammenitser Maggid), whose inspiration would uplift the people in their sadness and bring them hope for a happier future. He was a dedicated vegetarian, and even in the fog and slush of midwinter, he wore shoes made of cloth to show his abhorrence of leather. He taught them how to remain healthy on a small pittance, and brought beauty into their lives by teaching them compassion for all living creatures.

As a deeply religious man, he had a tremendous following. The crowds were such that even the traffic was held up when he preached in the streets. Learning of vegetarianism for the first time, and with her early traumatic experience, my mother vowed that when she grew up and had a family, she would bring them up as vegetarians.

My father came from Leczyca (pronounced Linchitz!) near Lodz, the Manchester of Poland, which was then part of Imperial Russia. His parents had an old, established textile warehouse, but at the tender age of fourteen they sent him on his own to London. They hoped that he would find some security in life and avoid spending thirteen years in the barbaric Tzarist army, from which so many never returned.

He was of an adventuresome and determined turn of mind, and having heard great tales of the freedom and beauty of England, decided when he was churned out into the seething cauldron of the East End that it was not for him. He discovered Toynbee Hall, which provided free education, and in due course mastered English perfectly. At this people's college he made friends with a Swiss man who invited him to come and live with him in the (then) delightful little fishing port of Poole, near Bournemouth. There he learned that there was an England outside of the East End and in due course progressed until he possessed the status symbol of those days — a gold-knobbed walking stick. Through an introduction he visited my mother in London, and she was duly impressed by the gold-knobbed walking stick.

He loved the little towns and the countryside so when they married they moved to Winchester, the ancient capital of Wessex. Later they moved to Salisbury in Wiltshire, then to Devizes and eventually to the Roman city of Bath in Somerset. We were four in the family, each born in a different town.

By now you will be wondering what all this has to do with vegetarianism. I will tell you!

Moving in those days meant the arrival of a great, lovely, old shaggy horse, with feet like pancakes, and behind it a long pant-echnicon. After packing, the breadwinner would mount alongside the driver and the long trek to the next town would commence. There was ample room inside the contraption for sleeping at night. Unlike now, every other house had rooms to let, so on arrival accommodation was easily secured. The rolls of lino would be duly laid on the floors, the necessary furniture erected, and perhaps to make it a little more attractive, the aspidistra in its jardiniere would be placed in position. A couple of days later the mother with the young family would take the train to the new place of abode.

And so it happened that on one of these perigrinations (from Salisbury to Devizes) my father was resting in his new habitat, tired and very hungry. He never believed in half measures, and believing that meat made him strong, was a very heavy meat eater. Already at the age of twenty-three his left shoulder was badly affected with rheumatism and he could hardly move the arm. The landlady had left the house to do some shopping and her supper was cooking in the kitchen. To use his own words, "the delicious smell of frying liver" proceeded from that sanctuary, and unable to resist, he crept in and gently lifted the lid covering the frying pan. As he gazed in awe at this slab of the animal's organ, he noticed it rising higher and higher, when all of a sudden it burst and from the ulcer, yellow pus ran all over the surface. He dashed back to his room feeling rather sick.

Vegetarian shops have always been noted for hiding their lights behind bushels, but in Devizes a young couple saw no reason for this reticence. They had made a public inconvenience of themselves by posting circulars through everybody's letter-box, with the wording, "Why live on dead and diseased flesh when you can purchase the delicious pure products of sun and air?" This, together, with the periodic nagging he had received from my mother, who had never forgotten her vow, made him betake himself to the address on the circular, and there he found a bright young man who gave him every help and encouragement.

As I have said, my father never did things in half measures so he carried back a tremendous package of goodies; fresh wholemeal bread, nut butters (such as you cannot get today), Pitman's delicious nut preparations, compressed fruit bars, etc. The next day my mother arrived, and before she had time to cross the threshold, he made the declaration, "Bluma, we have become vegetarians!" This was most unexpected, and I am informed that it was only the shock which caused her to start crying and ask, "Do you think the children will be well without even a little meat broth?"

Two years later I was born and that is why I am a vegetarian.

My wife was a "natural" and now enjoys helping the "Beauty Without Cruelty" movement. Our daughter, Vivien, who lives in Italy, is making much impact in a land which hitherto has looked upon meat as a status symbol.

I am grateful for the course that was set for me and consider it a privilege to play my part, however small, in exposing the fallacy and ugliness of the flesh-devouring habit. I am happy to do whatever is within my power to lessen the conflict and suffering arising from man's global war against creation.

Philip L. Pick

New Year Irresolution

EDITORIAL

". . .they shall not hurt nor destroy in all my holy mountain."

Unlike the hilarious and bacchanalian celebrations with which the Solar New Year is greeted, the approach of each year in the Jewish calendar is anticipated with awe, and a humble awareness that as each notch is marked up on the great tree of life, the all-pervading and predestined purpose of the universe will prevail.

To each individual, as a microcosm of creation, falls a minutia of responsibility in advancing or retarding universal progress, and each individual is aware of the part he is intended to play, even though more often than not, this awareness is deliberately relegated to the unthinking recesses of the mind, the better to avoid any diversion of everyday plans and desires. The universal celebration of this terrestrial measure of time indicates how closely our finite life is linked with infinite creation, and this individual responsibility for corporate action is publicly declared in our services by the use of the plural throughout.

"*We* have done violence—*we* have gone astray—*we* have led others astray—etc." The message is clear: the oft-heard excuse "If I don't, someone else will," is not acceptable. The units are the sum total of the whole.

In every synagogue, even in remote and unheard of corners of the world, congregations will assemble to render acknowledgement to the Creator, to examine the year that has past and to consider the year that lies ahead. Most will use the extended shopping list, requesting deliveries in the year to come. "Remove pestilence, sword and famine; hold back the plague; send perfect healing; have pity and compassion on us; fill our storehouses with plenty.

Shall we participate in the use of poisoned carcases of birds and beasts for food; and ask for a perfect healing? Above all shall we harden our hearts to the cries of tormented creatures reared in the captivity and darkness of factory farms; and ask for pity and compassion for ourselves and our infants?

Resolution, and a moiety of endeavour from each according to his ability, and understanding of the need, is the consideration due before the requests on the shopping list should be proffered. Each will find a different purpose for constructive effort and should surely apply themselves accordingly.

Those who understand the basis of vegetarian endeavour, comprehend that a great and beautiful building cannot be erected on unsound or rotting foundations. Love of humanity (whether they be adults or children), peace, sustenance, and good health, the common birthright of all peoples, cannot be achieved on the basis of the desire for flesh.

There are some who deny a divine purpose and therefore bear no individual responsibility. The question arises why such participate in this great universal declaration. Is it just herd instinct or the love of social gatherings? Is it a somewhat dishonest means of joining the queue for an annual fashion show with perhaps, who knows, the possibility of obtaining a share of the goodies on the shopping list?

Some, like habitual debtors demanding further supplies, will attend the holy convocation whilst breaking the prohibition of leather shoes, or will be bedecked in furs torn violently from defenceless animals whose breath of life had not yet departed.

Who will enter the New Year with irresolution, and who with firm resolve will contribute a minute share toward the age, however remote, when the flaming swords will be removed and all beings shall again enter their Garden of Eden to live forever at peace with their Maker?

"To Man and all creatures wherein there is a living soul." (Genesis)

"The Road To Hell. . .

EDITORIAL

. . .is paved with good intentions," and there is little doubt that men such as Bernard, Pasteur, Ehrlich and many others, had only the best of intentions when they pursued their studies, and laid the foundations for the present worldwide practice of vivisection.

We look for the day when the unfortunate practice of eating flesh will cease, and when the slaughterhouses that cover the fair face of the earth like scabs will be as obsolete as the Roman arena or the Inquisition.

Vivisection (in common with furs, skins, and tetanus-loaded fertilizers) is a "fringe benefit," an accessory or by-product, that completes the circle necessary to a way of life centered on the slaughterhouse. The formula for vegetarianism is basic and simple, it makes no reference to vivisection; the need for such unwholesome practice is eliminated. But it will be many years before the millions cease in their flesh-devouring habits. It is therefore gratifying that special organizations to combat the ever growing atrocities exist in many countries, and are dedicated and hard working. In Britain the campaign against vivisection gained momentum toward the end of the last century, and was ardently supported by the intelligentsia; including Bernard Shaw, Carlisle, Tennyson, Lind-af-Hageby and many others. From Scotland comes the greatest driving force; inspiration linked to efficiency is producing an impact far beyond the Scottish borders.

It is however, because experimentation on living creatures has become so widespread, with a total disregard for purpose or pity, that an expression of our own views is called for. The absence of a statement by a vegetarian journal dedicated to the ethical aspect could in some quarters be inferred as condoning the practice. Silence means assent; how can we remain silent when the muffled cries of a million sentient creatures defile the environment and darken the horizon with evil forebodings?

Many are worried; they feel that vivisection provides an umbrella protection against hostile biological forces, yet view the method with revulsion, and wander indecisively in a mental no-man's land.

Cleanliness or Ungodliness

The founders of this science did not or could not foresee the developments that would ensue; experimentation on a universal scale for many nonmedical purposes; a direction in thinking that would lead people away from the rightful path of health, and a demand by the multitude for instant protection against all possible ailments without effort on their own part. Undoubtedly the great drug cartels have assisted in this conditioning process until the experiments have become mystic and sacred: an image of sorcerers stirring their cauldrons of magic brew, dispensing their healing balm to the believers whilst leaving the "heretics" and their loved ones unguarded and open to annihilation by hordes of frightening two-headed long-toothed, stinging, biting bacteria, bringing agony and death to the infidel. These nightmares cause otherwise normal people to stampede for disinfectants, sterilizers, sprays, and injections, in a great war against the ever-present unseen limitless virus, and the larger enemies that creep, crawl, and fly in the night, whilst the example of millions of healthy, happy, long-lived, active, and disease-free communities pass unnoticed, with no questions asked as to why they are exempt.

It is not intended to consider the extent of knowledge resulting from animal experimentation, or the benefits, if any, that have accrued therefrom. We are dealing with basic principles. The claim to have eliminated thereby some of the more deadly diseases is based on assumption—which is wholly foreign to the proven accuracy scientists normally demand.

In medieval days the Black Plague spread across Europe decimating the populations of towns and villages. Miraculously, so it appeared, it passed over the heads of the Jewish population leaving it unharmed. Locked within ghettos dwelling in extreme congestion in high buildings fronting narrow streets, through which little air and no sun ever penetrated, one would have thought that they would have suffered more than those who lived a free and open life outside the ghetto gates. The medicos could not or would not understand this apparent contradiction. The mob, accusing the Jews of poisoning the wells, engaged in raging pogroms, causing more devastation with a stream of refugees in its wake.

Of course the answer was simple, the Jews strictly observed the ancient Hebrew Laws which detailed hygiene in food and habits, thus granting them complete immunity from the dreaded plague.

Even in an advanced country such as Britain , at the beginning of the century, open sewers, cesspits, and unfiltered water were still used. Hardly a vestige of control existed over the slaughter of diseased animals and the sale of infected carcasses.

In poor areas it was customary in the fall of the year to sew the children into their winter clothes, which were not removed until the following April or May, hence the adage "Cast not a clout 'til May's well out.' The living and the dead would often occupy the same room; infection of children's heads would be such that the hair would be seen to rise and fall with the movement of the lice. The stockpot was always on the boil, bones and bits of offal added from week to week; a cauldron of bacteria whose virulence was surely capable of wiping out a continent! The myth of this nourishing broth soon laid low the invalid with the mildest of maladies, and spread the plague with monotonous regularity.

Not surprising therefore that folk were struck down with contagious diseases, but surprising indeed that Jenner and his contemporaries lacked the vision to comprehend the real cause.

Serum or Self-repair

Was it beyond the scope of their gifted imaginations to realise that the good Lord could not have been so lacking in foresight as to construct man with no self-repairing outfit and therefore needing an injection before the work of creation could be considered complete?

The improvement in general hygiene is unquestioned, but it is the work of local authorities and general-health regulations that have caused the plague to abate and the reduction of the killer diseases. The part played by inoculation is exceedingly doubtful. Were it possible to ascertain the truth, which it is not, the number who perished or were maimed through inoculation-induced gangrene and encephalitis would be found to exceed the casualties arising from the original cause. It is not sufficiently known that live vaccine can cause disability at any time throughout life, and it is to the everlasting credit of the independently minded British people that it has not been possible to impose compulsory vaccination on them. When attempts were made this large minority took to rioting in the streets. Today we know that the word Thalidomide illumines only a very small tip of a large iceberg; the extent and seriousness of physical and mental derangements arising from injections lies hidden below the surface safe from the public gaze.

No evidence exists to show that those who were not inoculated suffered more than those who were so "protected." In fact the amazing silence of the authorities on this point leads one to think that the effect may be just the opposite. This has now been recognized in Britain, America, and other countries where vaccination is considered to be as great or greater a danger than the relevant diseases. The problem causes much distress as is evidenced by requests received by us for help, such as "I do not wish my baby to be vaccinated but am worried in case he catches an infection. What shall I do?" It is a difficult question to answer; our reply is invariably that we do not give advice on a highly professional subject but if a child is brought up free from the contaminations of decomposing flesh and with its fair share of protective natural raw foods, then the risk from inoculation would no doubt be greater than from any possible natural cause.

Rights or Responsibilities

It is not a matter of bookkeeping, of gain or loss, of setting advantages against disadvantages, or the balancing of human and animal suffering.

Sooner or later all events move inexorably to their climax. This century, experimentation on defenceless and innocent victims has escalated blindly with no adequate contemplation of the issues involved and with no consideration whatsoever for the ultimate ends.

Not a thought as to the limits of man's dominion, or the rights to which such creatures may be entitled. From whence derived the authority to condemn these subjects to fear, torture, and a lingering death; at what period of history was such authority granted? This question seems to have been avoided; the practice indicates an assumption of total and absolute power, a belief in a supreme and final hegemony, an unquestionable acceptance that man is the ultimate of all things on this earth with no liege or tutelage, answerable to no-one and responsible only to the expansiveness of his own imagination.

And what of the brutalization of youth at its most impressionable age, particularly of the unfortunate few who carry within them a latent tendency to sadism. The practice of dissection at an early age destroys all sensitivity and ensures that society will in due course be the recipient of the ultimate in violence and crime. The seed is being sown in schools throughout the world and a bitter harvest will be reaped.

There is no line of demarcation; the experimenter who straps a dog or other animal to the table and proceeds to test his conscious reactions must sooner or later feel the need to test a human body likewise. The opportunity to indulge this pent-up desire found full force in Nazi Germany when supplies of healthy Jewish prisoners, male and female, were sent to the vivisectors' laboratories to satisfy the curiosity of eminent German scientists. Now the bridge has been crossed and throughout the world experimentation on humankind is taking place without the knowledge or consent of the victim. The struggle is joined, the insensitivity bred in previous generations is coming to the surface, sadism has spread from the vivisectors' table to human relationships everywhere.

Safeguards have been bitterly fought for and are somewhat better in Britain than most other countries though inspection is ineffective and sedation in many cases would hamper the object of the experiment. The cost is massive, substantial sums are received from foundations provided by the drug companies and levies of government taxes from health, education, and other departments. Antivivisectionists, vegans, and vegetarians alike also contribute their full share to its upkeep whether they desire it or not. A close involvement of commercial firms facilitates government approval of the chemical products and subsequent success of the sales programme.

It is an even greater moral issue whether this research shall be conducted for nonmedical purposes; warfare, the space programme, and the testing of chemical additives and cosmetics. In the latter case it is particularly inexcusable, bearing in mind the unlimited supply of fragrant natural and beautifying plant products, which are so readily available and so beneficial and kind to the user. The inducement of gradual blindness and the causation of skin cancers are wholly inexcusable and result from sheer commercial greed. It is a sobering thought that in France orphans are used for the testing of chemical cosmetics.

Retribution or Reward

It is also a moral question as to the continuation of these practices, when results have already been ascertained, and when such results can be supplied to students without need for repetitive experimentation. Or when viable and more accurate means of testing are immediately available, such as computerization, tissue cells, and plastic models for demonstration and dissection purposes.

The cost has to be counted; the resultant departure from natural living and natural safeguards has produced astronomical expenditure and a National Health Service collapsing beneath a crippling financial burden. If a minute proportion of the money, ingenuity, and time, spent on this creed of "knowledge through torture" were devoted to prevention, the benefit to the community both in health and economics would be profound. Scope for the future advancement of hygiene is still unlimited; airborne lead and sulphur and polluted food from poisoned earth are readily preventable. Simple research in this sphere would yield a harvest of health which a million creatures in their slow agonizing death could never achieve.

The time is late—too late for neutrality. Each must make his

own decision as to the world he wants to see. A world in which
disease, drugs, and surgery thrive on a pagan philosophy, where
the weak and the voiceless are trampled upon, or a world in which
health shall spring from the vital cleansing protective powers yielded
up from the priceless gifts of the earth, and harmony shall be
achieved through respect for all life.

"His tender mercies are over all his works." The Torah is concerned about pain caused to animals because they lack knowledge
and intelligence to endure suffering, whereas man can choose to
cast his mind and to accept with love whatever befalls him. Some
may think that this subject is irrelevant to the great human problem
of today, but the infliction of suffering on the helpless, either
human or animal, brings certain retribution. Through the practice
of compassion we may merit the divine reward and thus help to
restore the blessings of peace, health and harmony.

"And in that day will I make covenant for them with the beasts
of the field and with the fowls of heaven and with the creeping
things of the ground. And I will break the bow and the sword and
the battle out of the land and I will make them to lie down safely."

Hosea 2.20

Of Cabbages and Cows

EDITORIAL

(With Apologies to ALICE IN WONDERLAND)

"The time has come, the Walrus said,
'To talk of many things;
Of shoes — and ships — and sealing-wax —
Of cabbages — and kings."

Whenever the season of midsummer madness is with us, it is good to spend a few hazy lazy moments dwelling on the ubiquitous quality of nonsense.

In the Victorian era it was a highly respected art form but fell into a decline at the turn of the century, probably due to the spread of universal education, which happy facility, seems to lessen the sense of humour and induce a somewhat more (or more than somewhat) seriousness of temperament.

On closer consideration however, it is evident that reams of nonsense are still being written and spoken, but a gullible public is unable to recognize it as such and treats it as serious matter. Theoreticians and superficial opportunists (one hesitates to call them cranks, which epithet has long since earned the right to honourable title) peddle obscure remedies for age-old problems to which the human race has always been heir. These writers have profundity thrust upon them by otherwise honourable literary critics, and who, by serious criticisms mask the nonsense with a cloak of earnestness, thus encouraging such efforts, whether the writers be possessed of an elementary knowledge of the subject or not.

In the past few years for example, even medical and scientific works used to adjudge that health could only be maintained by the macabre practice of carnivourism and which should be practiced three times a day to rebuild body wastage. Now this has proved to be arrant nonsense, the current crop of hoodwinkers have been hard pressed to find other aspects to help the multitude in their reluctance to release the lifeless bodies into which their teeth are well and truly fastened. The current craze is the much heralded discovery that there is consciousness in plant life, and which responds to electronic impulses. A great revelation for the atomic age! Not without purpose has the world evolved through these past millenniums to have at last reached such a state of intellectuality and to conceive of such an epoch-making discovery.

It is of course possible that those who write on such pro-fundities may well be laughing up their sleeves as the royalties come rolling in. They must be fully aware that these mysteries have been known in every generation, and that it is but a gimmick to equate plant vibrations with conscious emotional animal existence to satisfy twentieth-century ethics. It is a useful argument against the ever-growing number of woolley-headed vegetable eaters. After all if it is just as cruel to kill a cabbage as a cow, then why become vegetarian?

Of course the real logic is avoided, as well it should be in all true nonsense. It is impossible to comprehend the myriad life forms that must exist in, around, and through every part of the material and nonmaterial spheres in which we exist. Zoroastra succinctly wrote: "Consciousness sleeps in the minerals, begins to stir in the plant world and awakes to full consciousness in the animal kingdom."

Solomon, the wisest of men, is reputed to have understood the language of animals and birds, but not of the flowers and trees. In Ireland the "little people," the guardian angels of the plants, have been seen around for many centuries, and heaven help the person who tells an Irishman that it is only his imagination resulting from a drop too much to drink. In sentimental England, hard-headed and practical personalities have written books about the fairies that live at the bottom of their gardens, and who would dare to deny the mystery of green fingers, which is so ably demonstrated by garden lovers everywhere.

Undoubtedly plant life sends out vibrations, as definite as those which emanate from a vacant house, long occupied, but now deserted, with its eerie impact of sorrow or happiness absorbed into its fabric by residents long since departed.

But vibrations are something different from the consciousness of our sentient kith and kin; our blood brothers whose evolved being is polarized in the brain, and who like ourselves, know love, hate, fear, and jealousy. Who rear their young with a deep affection often exceeding that found among their human betters, and who have legs wherewith to run from fear and danger. Whose tongues, like our own, communicate with each other and cry when they suffer pain or grief or terror, even as we do. Whose mute and soulful eyes plead for love, companionship, and pity. Who conceivably may convey their silent prayers to the same creator, and who, even though the prayers may be unanswered, may, in the obscurity of our understanding, keep abiding faith. For does not our Sabbath morning service commence with the words "The soul of every living creature shall bless thy name"?

We comprehend the miracle of creation and observe all things adapted to their purpose. We see plant life covering the surface of the earth, immobile, an elementary continuous nerve system with no brain polarization, that the quality of pain shall be nonexistant. A primitive organization for the synthesis of radiation, providing an abundant production of food seed, and a copious recurring growth of green leaves. Wonderously adapted to gather moisture in dry heat, yielding cold, sweet thirst-quenching fruits where no water is found. Tree formations attracting clouds, sheltering the bare earth from the scorch of the midday sun and profuse in the provision of sustenance. Is not all this clearly ordained and defined in Genesis?

The fallacy of linking plant and animal life in common suffering is a desecration of our teachings and a confusion to rightful thinking. It creates a dangerous diversion of logic, and not only justifies the slaughter of animals for food, but by the same reasoning, could regularize cannibalism or the consumption of the aged, the imbecile, and the excess of population in the human race. The elite of Rome's imperial palaces would pay homage to the beauty of flowers whilst the slaves were burned in the market places, and nearer to our day those at the pinnacle of the Nazi hierarchy, would lovingly caress a beloved kitten, and with a bayonet butt, smash the skull of a Jewish or Gypsy child in the presence of its mother.

The futile sensation seeking experimentation on plant consciousness is not always innocently promoted. We believe that the cartels of the slaughter industry are no less active than in the days of Upton Sinclair, and this form of perverted thought serves well their purpose, to vindicate the breeding, imprisonment, and slaughter of all those highly developed conscious creatures whose birthright is to be born free, to graze the hills and valleys, drink the pure cold water of the mountain streams, and feel the warmth of the sun and the cooling rain.

There is a gradation in life; let not the roaming imagination of the human mind attribute to awakening plant life the same measure of consciousness as the beast of the field, or man who climbs, falteringly may be, rung by rung of the heavenly ladder.

Let vegetarians, ecologists, and all those who are working for a saner world, avoid spreading this grossly misleading concept, less they help perpetrate carnivourism with its corollary of human starvation and misery.

The equation of plant and animal life is but a caricature of the mind, and those who have been able to retain that most uncommon gift of common sense will recognize it as a form of nonsense that should find a place on the bookshelves alongside the works of Edward Lear and Lewis Carroll.

Festival of Freedom

EDITORIAL

"For lo, the winter is passed, the rain is over and gone;
flowers appear on the earth; the time of singing of birds is
come. . . ." Song of Songs

These beautiful words were written in anticipation of a long Summer
in Israel, but this article is being penned in London, where the rain
and the sleet still beat on the window panes; the earth is still cold,
and the slanting rays of the sun are as yet too weak to entice the tightly
folded buds to open out into a colourful welcome for the approaching
Spring.

Mother Earth slowly awakens, breathing life into unseen forms
and charging the elements with mystical regenerative powers. The
human mind, too, free from the sluggish pall of Winter, gains new
impetus to search, to enquire, and to create.

At the appointed time, Passover, the Festival of Freedom,
heralds the changing season with a clarion call to arise and shake off
Winter's bondage of sloth and despondency; to beathe in deeply of
the new life, new health, spiritual awareness that pervades the
atmosphere with the changing season.

Not alone is the Passover a mode of diet for eight days, neither
is it merely a recital from history or a restatement of religious and
ethical beliefs. The elimination of all leaven to commemorate the

emergence from bondage carries a clear message for humanity at large. An eternal message that man and all creatures for time everlasting are endowed with the basic need and unquenchable love of freedom. The slave of many years emerging from his darkened cell into the light of day may find it difficult indeed to change his prison ways, and the millions who have found themselves in chains of their own making will not find it easy to loosen the shackles of unthinking habit and mental atrophy; even in the dim twilight of their own inurement, they will surely feel at this season the earth's emerging soul bringing inspiration and the call to action.

Clearly the Passover message is a summons for slumbering minds to awake, to attune themselves to the pulsating heart of the Universe and to re-establish the ever-diminishing quality of freedom. But not alone the freedom from man's oppression of man, this would but mean the freedom to exploit and destroy other forms of life at will. The absence of leaven is a call for self-denial, not an encouragement to even greater obscenities in diet via a circuitous legal defile.

It is not a call to gorge on kugel, kreplech, kneidlich, kishgars, kutchgas, puddings, plavas, pancakes, petits fours, chocolate, chrane, biscuits, blintzes, latkes, lockshen, schmaltz, schnitzels, and schnappes. It is a festival of regeneration, not decimation. All the admixtures, the processes, the alchemy, the frying, the baking, the boiling, the mashing, the infusing and the diffusing, cannot but produce an element of leaven, and such culinary contortions are used but to avert the simple decree. All but the adherents of the cult of the stomach religion will understand unequivocally that the object of being completely free of leaven is to cleanse the body, thus fitting it for mental and spiritual release. The prohibition clearly indicates an eight-day period of return to natural living, the fruits of the tree and the green herbs of the field and a lesson to learn so that the spirit of Springtime will last throughout the coming year.

"Remember you were slaves in Egypt"—the lesson of slavery applies in its widest form. The slavery of the stomach necessitates the slavery of the cooking pot, the slavery of the cook spending beautiful Spring days chopping, mixing, stirring, and steaming over the cooking stove, altering and destroying the thrilling flavours and cleansing properties of the natural gifts of the earth. The slavery of countless millions of gentle creatures, fellow occupants of this planet, denied the joy of the Spring grass and the sunshine, the young removed from the terrified mothers, and imprisoned in darkness; frightened in life and diseased in death to grace the table for the festival of freedom. The slavery of the farmer tending day and night to the needs and wants of his multitude of enslaved creatures, nursing the sick, inseminating, attending births, milking, feeding, day and night without end; not the rest from toil which comes with the fallow land or the changing duties and the joy which comes from the changing season, but only everlasting servitude as a prison warder. Here then is the sting, a festival of freedom where liberty is denied and which death defiles.

And if these aspirations prove too difficult to achieve in everyday life, shall we not use the freedom of the coming vacation period, be it only for a brief week or two, to break the bounds of our confinement and fly away, not to the forests of concrete or the jungles where the roar of the internal combustion engines wreak their havoc, and where numerous hordes of faceless creatures push and hustle albeit without the order and dignity of the antheap; for this lesson of freedom indicates the need to tear away from the triviality of thoughts and competitive jealousies, from the image of self-importance, the practice of self-pity and trivia *ad nauseum*; to depart from the bazaar and the caravan route, the noisome bargaining and the minor intrigue; to take the way which leads to the isolation of the hills, the dunes and the forests, there to find humble abode, sweet food from the earth and sweet sweet sleep resulting from daytime exertions in the sun; there to breathe deeply the breath of life, feeling the wind on the cheek and to stride forth to the pulsating quietness of God's handiwork. Thus shall the spirit each day give greater strength and carry one further afield until even those who are supported with sticks shall throw them aside; the crutches of the mind, too, shall be cast away and the spirit of the creative Universe shall be inhaled, giving back understanding and freedom to the soul.

This, then, is the real meaning of Passover, even though it lasts but eight days, the grinding of the great city shall henceforth be but a shadow play; the selfish antagonisms of semicivilised hordes, visions of human starvation and warfare, the horrors of abattoirs, the sight of corpses hanging in the shops for human food, all this and the pounding of devilish engines around our ears may lurk in the mind's recesses, but the festival of freedom truly observed will carry the spirit above this man-made hell on earth, to fly with the winds and winged creatures, to understand the omniscient activity of life's cycle fulfilling myriad duties to complete the earthly purpose.

For each individual is as a slave in Egypt and by his own efforts alone shall he become free.

Horses

By Melech Ravitch — 1919

(Translated by Shulamis Yelin)

(Melech Ravitch was one of the great contemporary Yiddish writers
and poets whose work will preserve for posterity the treasures of
Yiddish literature.)

Many today will not remember the age of horse transport; great
kindly creatures fighting with unnatural loads, usually whipped and
cursed by the drivers. This poem brings back vividly those days, and
indeed the nonchanging pattern of man's ingratitude.

Full eighteen years they lugged their load
Forgotten, lonely, a pitiful pair;
Full eighteen years, in a stall by the bridge
Dust robbed the lustre from their hair.

Full eighteen years they suffered the lash
which anguished and shrivelled their aching hide,
and honestly earned their meagre repast
of straw at noon and eventide.

One night as they both stood, raindrenched and chilled,
the older one coughed, and pressed his head

to his sorrowing brother, confessed: "My friend,
I am tired and weary, and would I were dead.

Full eighteen years of silent woe
we've labored — light forsakes the eye.
Our knees tremble, our bodies swell,
and time runs dry."

Then, once in the night, as they mutely looked down
those two lonely brothers, for comfort in vain,
their master, in pub, drove a bargain sound
with a butcher from town.

They shook hands on the deal
with cash as a brand
on the lonely flesh
of the lonely land.

The bargain included
one long last ride,
one last great load
from the country-side.

And as in the previous eighteen years
they lumbered beneath the lash of the whip,
they dragged for his comfort on long winter's nights
split logs, on their very last trip.

And on their return, no noonday's repast,
to deaden their weariness, hushed in the fold,
then sadly, unwittingly, trundled their bones
to the slaughter-house cold.

And sensing the blood from the slaughterer's floor,
both animals trembled, and wearily bent,
their bony heads locked in last loving embrace,
stood scenting their end.

And when he untied the horrible yoke
from their oppressed and outraged shapes,

there lay the blackness of eighteen years
scourged into the anguished hairless napes.

And doused in the blood from the slaughterer's floor
echoed the roar of their clattering feet
on rattling iron of answering bridge,
sounding, resounding in silent street.

It recalled their full measure, on cobbles of yore,
in woods and in hamlet, on turf and on sod,
eighteen long years in a desolate world,
two lonely, forlorn creatures of God.

The Life of His Beast

Rabbi Everett E. Gendler

Charles Darwin was not the first human being to posit a close relation between man and the other animals. He may have put this particular notion to new theoretical use, he may have made our sense of kinship with other animals function differently in this particular age from the way it did in the centuries preceding. But the fact is that man's sense of relatedness to other living creatures is a very ancient inheritance of the human species. The 104th Psalm and the 148th Psalm express clearly the Psalmist's close identification not only with human life but also with the entire life of the Universe, even as it expresses itself in the lives of the beasts of the field, the monsters of the deep, and the birds of the air.

Nor is this simply an accident of the Book of Psalms. Those of you who are familiar with the creation story in Genesis have perhaps noticed that the sea animals and the birds which fly receive the same blessings as men: "be fruitful and multiply."[1] One notices also that beasts of the earth as well as men are invited to the banquet provided by the herbs, fruits, and growths of the earth's surfaces.[2] One notices even that the important Hebrew term *nephesh chaya* — which means "a living being" or "a living soul" — is applied both to animals and to man in the creation story in Genesis.[3] Granted, man in some respects, surpasses the capacities of the animals; Genesis is explicit about this. But the basic relatedness is not lost sight of even with the awareness of difference.

Nor is this sense of kinship confined simply to sentiments for singing on occasions of worship. The five Books of Moses include a number of specific laws dealing with proper treatment of the other animals, for they too are creatures of the Divine and objects of His express concern. To mention a few of them briefly: "You may not muzzle an ox as it threshes the grain."[4] The grain looks good to it? Let it eat! It must not be subjected to the frustration of facing food while it works and is itself muzzled. "Lo tachsom." Don't muzzle the ox as it threshes. And this was extended by rabbinic interpretation to other animals, even birds, working within sight of food.[5]

Another example: Even at the time when the sacrificial cult was practiced, it was forbidden to take a newborn ox, sheep, or goat from the mother until it had at least seven days of warmth and nourishment directly from its mother.[6] The idea that a newborn sacrifice is superior was rejected by the Bible lest there be the immediate theft of the offspring from the warm suckling of the mother.

There are other provisions, including the commandment that we're all familiar with: "Remember the Sabbath day and keep it holy. Six days you shall labor and do all your work, but the seventh day is a sabbath of the Lord your God: you shall not do any work—you, your son or daughter, your male or female slave, or your cattle, or the stranger who is within your settlements."[7] Less famous but even more significant is the provision in Exodus, Chapter 23: "Six days you shall do your work, but on the seventh day you shall cease from labor, in order that your ox and your ass may rest, and that your bondman and the stranger may be refreshed."[8] Here the Sabbath is proclaimed not only for the sake of man but for the sake of the animals as well!

All of this could be summed up in the saying in Proverbs: vo-de-a tza-dik ne-fesh b'hem-to, "the decent man considers the life of the beast."[9]

Nor is the motion confined in the West only to the Jewish tradition. One of the great figures of Western culture is surely Francisca of Assisi, called St. Francis by the Church. Many of you are undoubtedly familiar with St. Francis' great friendship with other creatures, and you probably recall that St. Bonaventure, in *The Life of St. Francis*, mentions that when Francis "bethought himself of the first beginning of all things, he was filled with a yet more overflowing charity, and would call the dumb animals, howsoever small, by the names of brother and sister, forasmuch as he recognized in them the same origin as in himself."[10] And many of you, I'm sure, are also aware of the provision in The Mirror of Perfection which St. Francis urges upon the emperor: "to make a law that men should make a good provision for birds and oxen and asses and the poor at Christmas-time," with a specification thereof.[11]

It is against this background of biblical and traditional Western religious concern for all living creatures, then, that I want briefly to view this new development: so-called factory farming or intensive rearing. What do the terms mean? Not simply the use of machines in farming, nor the striving for efficiency as such, but rather the uncritical application of technology to animal rearing so that animals, admittedly useful to man, are not regarded as fellow creatures.

It's an enterprise with which many of you are surely more familiar than I, but the effect on the observer is quite shocking. My own awareness of the development dates from a couple of years ago when my wife and I were in Maine, driving along a country road at night, and discovered time and again buildings, multistoried, with light shining from them, looking very much like urban apartment dwellings. Yet there were no signs of any other habitations around, no sizeable towns on the map, and it was very puzzling. A couple of days later, walking along a country road, we came upon one such building by daylight and discovered that a door was open. There was netting across the opening, making sure that none of the "contents" of the structure would spill out, and we saw crowded against the netting, piled on top of one another, countless numbers of chickens. From an elevated vantage point we were able to discern that this particular structure contained tens of hundreds of chickens, most of them in a semigloom, barely visible, obviously enclosed permanently. We were rather horrified by this forceable enclosure of beings who, however "low" on the evolutionary scale, presumably are gifted with flesh, blood, and at least a rudimentary sensory apparatus. For it is now the case that millions of animals spend their entire lives in darkness or semidarkness, without any free exposure to the natural elements, crowded together in pitiless fashion, subsisting but hardly living.

". . .day-old chicks are installed, eight or ten thousand at a time, sometimes more, in long, windowless houses punctuated only with extractor fans in surried rows along the ridge of the roofs, and air intake vents along the side walls. . . .Inside a house the impression is of a long, wide, dark tunnel disappearing into the gloom, the floor covered with chickens as far as the eye can see."[13]

And the results? . . . .the battery chickens I have observed seem to lose their minds about the time they would normally be weaned by their mothers and off in the weeds chasing grasshoppers on their own account. Yes, literally, actually, the battery becomes a gallinaceous madhouse. The eyes of these chickens through the bars gleam like those of maniacs. Let your hand get within reach and it receives a dozen vicious pecks not the love peck or the tentative peck of idle curiosity bestowed by the normal chicken, but a peck that means business, a peck for flesh and blood, for which in their madness they are thirsting. They eat feathers out of each other's backs or, rather, pull out each other's feathers and nibble voraciously at the roots of the same for tiny blocks of flesh and blood that may adhere thereto."[13]

Thus feather-pecking and cannibalism replace the normal "pecking order" of the farmyard. And the "solutions" to these technologically created problems? Not the establishment of conditions of life considerate of the instinctual needs of these creatures, but rather debeaking, reduced light, the fitting of opaque "specs" which prevent the chicken from seeing directly in front of it, cages, etc.

Please notice that I am not raising the issue of a few technological improvements, nor am I raising the issue of food production, though that is a consideration. Neither am I raising the question of the ultimate end of these animals, slaughter for human food, though that also is a question. I am rather asking that in the light of our religious heritage we face the question posed by Ruth Harrison on *Animal Machines*: "How far have we the right to take our domination of the animal world? Have we the right to rob them of all pleasures in life simply to make more money more quickly out of their carcasses? Have we the right to treat living creatures solely as food converting machines? At what point do we acknowledge cruelty?"[14] In the words of St. Francis, even while they live, how in fact are we treating our "brothers and sisters" who help sustain us? In the words of Proverbs, how are we regarding the lives of our beasts?

Listen to the terms we use now. As Ruth Harrison points out, the animal terms *hens* and *chickens* have become changed to such terms as *capons*, a marketably profitable result of hormonal distortion, or *broilers*, a term descriptive of the end result of creatures whose living identity no longer matters to us.

Listen to this quotation from a technical journal:

> The modern layer is, after all, only a very efficient converting machine, changing the raw materials—feeding stuffs—into the finished product—the egg—less, of course, maintenance requirements.[15]

And such examples can be brought in relation to veal calves, milk cows, and other animals whose very animality is disregarded in this one-dimensional viewing of them as mere food machines.

And please let's dispell a certain kind of technological provincialism. Technology has never before on this planet been developed to its present heights. But there was awareness long ago of the fact that if you let an animal run around, part of the energy which could go into eggs or milk or flesh for consumption is dissipated. It's interesting that there is a discussion by a medieval Jewish commentator in which he asks whether the provisions for resting the beast on the Sabbath mean that you simply rest the beast while being permitted to keep it enclosed, or whether this requires that the beast be permitted to graze freely on the farmland, nibbling the grass, etc. And the opinion of the commentator is that because the Bible uses the term "that your beast enjoy," it is required that it be permitted free grazing.[16] All of which suggests that the calculations we make and can act on with greater efficiency in our age are not unique to our age. The most significant difference between previous ages and our own may be that while they to some extent regarded the lives of their beasts, we seemingly manage to ignore them almost completely.

"To some extent, as the Minister is so fond of telling us, farm animals have always been exploited by man in that he rears them specifically for food. But until recently they were individuals, allowed their birthright of green fields, sunlight, and fresh air; they were allowed to forage, to exercise, to watch the world go by, in fact to live. Even at its worst, with insufficient protection against inclement weather or poor supplementation of natural food, the animal had some enjoyment in life before it died. Today the exploitation has been taken to a degree which involves not only the elimination of all enjoyment, the frustration of almost all natural instincts, but its replacement with acute discomfort, boredom, and the actual denial of health. It has been taken to a degree where the animal is not allowed to live before it dies."[17]

Let me briefly suggest also that if we were to look closely at the issue, it might even occur to us that the issue of respect for animals is really the issue of respect for life as such. Great seers such as Gandhi and Schweitzer also suggest that life is a continuum, and that one cannot make arbitrary cuts anywhere in the chain without doing injury at all levels. The least that Darwinism should mean for rational man is that, in a continuum, orientation toward one level of life will affect orientation toward all other levels of life. The issue of treatment of His beasts is, I suspect, in a subtle way also the issue of the treatment of other human beings and ourselves as well. There are those who have noticed that the sound of the planet is somewhat different now from what it used to be. St. Francis heard the songs of the beasts in praise of the Lord, and the psalmist recites his extravagant poetry with the accompanying sounds of all Creation praising Him, the Creator of all life. Our own ears seem to hear only the whir of machinery, not only as once in cities and factories, but now increasingly in the mangers of the beasts and the nests of the feathered ones, and this, I think, poses yet another part of the grave problem for us.

I want to conclude with a story about one of the Hasidic rabbis, Reb Zusya:

Once Rabbi Zusya traveled cross-country collecting money to ransom prisoners. He came to an inn at a time when the innkeeper was not at home. He went through the rooms, according to his custom, and in one saw a large cage with all kinds of birds. And Zusya saw that the caged creatures wanted to fly through the spaces of the world and be free birds again. He burned with pity for them and said to himself: "Here you are, Zusya, walking your feet off to ransom prisoners. But what greater ransoming of prisoners can there be than to free these birds from their prison?" Then he opened the cage, and the birds flew out into freedom.

When the innkeeper returned and saw the empty cage, he was very angry, and asked the people in the house who had done this to him. They answered: "A man is loitering about here and he looks like a fool. No one but he can have done this thing." The innkeeper shouted at Zusya: "You fool! How could you have the impudence to rob me of my birds and make worthless the good money I paid for them?" Zusya replied: "You have often read and repeated these words in the psalm: 'His tender mercies are over all His works.' " Then the innkeeper beat him until his hand grew tired and finally threw him out of the house. And Zusya went his way serenely.[18]

The conditions of captivity are different and the requirement for freeing the birds and other animals perhaps less radical. But their captors today will not initially smile at any attempt to reopen the cages, and those so concerned will seem, like Reb Zusya and St. Francis, rather strange and somewhat queer creatures. There will be verbal beatings, and out of many an agricultural establishment and academic department we are likely to be tossed unceremoniously. But I would nonetheless suggest that if ever again on this anguished planet we are to realize that His tender mercies do indeed extend over all His works, even human creatures; and if ever again we are to sing a full hymn of praise to the Creator of all Life, then somehow all of us must ourselves regain, and help our society itself regain, some considerable regard for the lives of our beasts.

 1. Genesis 1:22.
 2. Genesis 1:30.
 3. Genesis 1:20, 21, 24.
 4. Deuteronomy 25:4.
 5. Rashi, citing Talmud Baba Metziah 94b in support.
 6. Leviticus 22:27.
 7. Exodus 20:8-10.
 8. Exodus 23:12.
 9. Proverbs 12:10.
10. Ch. VIII Sec. 6.
11. Sec. XII Ch. CXIV.
12. Ruth Harrison *Animal Machines* (London, 1964, Vincent Street
    Ltd.) p. 12.
13. Ibid., pp. 154-55.
14. Ibid., p. 3.
15. Ibid., p. 50.
16. Rashi on Exodus 23:12.
17. Harrison, op. cit. p. 3.
18. *Tales of the Hasidim* by Martin Buber, Volume I, p. 249.

Cannibals and Carnivores

By Vivien Pick

(Vivien Pick, a Doctor of Music, is a third generation vegetarian and was the originator of the Jewish Vegetarian Society.)

How shocked and self-righteous we become when we learn that cannibalism still exists in many parts of the world — Africa, Australia, Polynesia, and South America, but to what degree is our civilisation superior? We make wars, kill and eat animal flesh; then in our smug self-approval we seek the blessing of our Creator.

Just so does the cannibal — but he does not like making war and is less hypocritical than ourselves about the whole business of killing. Primitive he may be, but the cannibal often has a clearer notion of ethics than we.

Some interesting sidelights into the cannibal mind are given in Volbard's *Cannibalism*.

"There is no difference — meat is meat. Everything that has life is the same. It's food to eat."

"Meat is meat" is a favourite self-justification when confronted with white man's accusations. It is a matter of where you decide to draw the line, whether as a society or an individual.

"I do not interfere when you kill a goat — why do you interfere when I kill a slave?"

"You eat animals of a low order, whereas we eat man, the most noble of animals. Therefore you are degenerate, not we."

Another cannibal reply to European indignation is rather the same as that given by white carnivores to their fellow vegetarians:

"This is our tradition. Our fathers and forefathers have always done so, and we must continue. Should we give up what we were taught as children?" Also: "Yes, we do eat man-flesh. But only a *little*." Or again: "But we only eat arms and legs."

Cannibals claim that human meat is superior to the animal variety in every way. This may or may not be true, but they certainly show a better physique and a higher level of intelligence than their neighbouring carnivore tribes. These quotations are all faithful reports as brought back by explorers and anthropologists, yet they could hardly show more similarity to the psychological processes of the "average" European carnivore.

The specific importance given by cannibals to human flesh banquets, and the excitement and revelry attached to such an occasion, can only be compared to the white man's "slaying the fatted calf" or roasting a whole ox for a special celebration. Cannibals are superstitiously attached to the idea of the special powers and virtues in human flesh. They believe it gives them the strength and qualities of the person eaten, just as we think that one can gain strength from beef (as strong as an ox.) In "civilized" society if an individual does not eat a particular food, for example potatoes or cheese due to personal dislike, no one pays overmuch attention to his preference, and certainly no one worries for his survival. But should one simply claim not to eat animal flesh, then the carnivores' reaction is extreme. They immediately presume that something vital is missing, that one will lack strength and resistance, and above all that one's children will not grow well.

These are precisely the same attributes the cannibal seeks in this horrible food. Like the carnivore, he immediately becomes suspicious. When it is suggested to him that one can live without this form of nourishment, he goes on the defensive and shows all the signs of mental stress that is shown by a drug addict when threatened with withdrawal of his drug, or the average European carnivore threatened with withdrawal of animal flesh. Indeed, all scholars agree that human flesh, animal flesh, and drugs show the same tendency to addiction in their consumers.

Leo Frobenius observed that primitives eat human flesh with the same attitude that "civilised" man eats a "good beef-steak"— there is the same emotional dependence and sense of extreme satiety afterwards. Even the most carnivorous of anthropologists concedes that the effect of human flesh on a cannibal is identical to that of animal flesh on a white man. This intoxication or addictive element in flesh is proved by the fact that in the only areas where cannibalism has been successfully eliminated (mainly in Angola) by providing a substitute, it has been replaced by the cultivation and use of cannabis (marijuana) or opium. The natives admit that they are content with the change, as the drugs produce the same euphoria as an orgy of flesh-eating.

Gluttony is one of the chief causes of cannibalism, as of carnivourism, especially as it rarely occurs in areas where food is really scarce. It is universally held that human flesh has such an extraordinarily exquisite flavour, that white man simply does not know what he is missing.

"You would eat man-meat too, if you only knew how good it was." The flavours of different tribes are discussed with all the concern of gourmets comparing the merits of their favourite dishes.

"The Bayakkas, who only eat the Lukkus, taste better than the Badingas, who only eat the Kukuangas."

In the most distant part of the globe, it is known that white man makes bad meat, due to his diet. White man's flesh is considered to have a bitter or oversalty taste, and indeed in South America several cannibals died after eating shipwrecked mariners in the last century. Queensland aborigines preferred a nice dish of Chinese flesh—the sweetest of all, due to the almost exclusively vegetable diet of the Chinese peasant.

There is much fascinating information about cannibal habits and beliefs, which cannot be included here, as it is not relevant to their relationship with their fellow corpse-eaters.

One point, however, is worth a final note.

There are cannibals in East Africa who like to "mature" their meat in water, or by burying it for several days. ("Hanging" game to make it "high"?)

Agnon: Teller of Tales

Shmuel Yosef Agnon, for many years a native of Talpiot in Jerusalem, hailed from Galicia and enjoyed the remarkable experience of becoming world famous when an octogenarian. His home, set in a pine garden next to the homes of the late Leib Jaffe and the late Professor Klausner, the great Jewish historian, was a quiet, creative corner; even with the bullets whizzing about the neighbourhood just before the siege of Jerusalem, these three men would go walking, ignoring the pot-shots while they were absorbed in conversation.

Mr. Agnon was in his house in 1928 when it was bombed but he was not wounded: his humane pity was not affected, and this dreadful experience never warped his warm friendship for the Arabs. The next year the Agnons built a new home on the adjacent plot. Austerely furnished the Agnon home was rich with treasures of Jewish manuscripts and books and ancient records, even of their own family for several centuries. Above all, it was a home steeped in religious observance. The Sabbath aura embraced the whole family and over the Holy Day each week their six grandchildren and their parents came to stay.

In 1913 he left for Germany to lecture on Hebrew literature. There he met Professor Moshe Marx (later on the staff of the Jewish Theological Seminary in New York), brother of his bride-to-be. The future Mrs. Agnon, who had already visited Palestine and planned to return one day, was studying Arabic in order to be able to communicate with the native population. She became so proficient in the field that eventually she taught the language. The Agnons married in 1920 and returned to the Holy Land four years later with their little girl, Emuna (Faith), and son, Hemdat (Joy). Mrs. Agnon turned into her husband's guardian, aware of his genius. Of frail build, her age almost matching her husband's, her mind is as active as his, and charm and goodness emanate from her just as from her husband. No wonder Mr. Agnon referred to his wfe as "my love," it was no empty courtly phrase. For she shared with him every iota both of his personal and creative life, even acting as his scribe in "those days" and his typist until their daughter took over. "The only role I wanted to fill in life was to be my husband's wife." But she is also his fan. "I love almost all of his works now as I always have."

Though his works are now world-acclaimed, his genius has rarely been glimpsed by the non-Jewish public. Gifted in writing from his early years, at the age of fiteen he already had stories published in newspapers and soon after in book form. Coming to Israel as an idealist in 1908 he lived through the Turkish regime, the British mandate, the founding of the Jewish State, and enjoyed a rewarding life there.

On the occasion of his becoming an Honorary Fellow of the Weizmann Institute, at the meeting of its Board of Governors held at the Wix Auditorium in Rehovat, he said: "Two precious gifts has the Holy One, Blessed be He, given to men of His choice: the study of the spirit of man and the telling of His doings; and the study of the world and the fullness thereof. The study of the soul of man and his deeds He has entrusted to the tellers of tales; the secrets of the earth and the study of the material world with all its ramifications, He has entrusted to the sages of science. Which of the two is the better? He who tells what he has seen and heard; or he who tells what he is shown and what he is made to hear? There were two men in our town, to whom I was drawn throughout the days of my infancy. One was a scribe of sacred writings; the other was a smith. Whenever it was possible I would watch them at their work, and my eyes were never sated with looking. Actually they were very different from each other in the things they did, but my mind's eye made them into one entity, and combined the two doers into one body engaged in two crafts. The one lived in a little house near the klios of the Hassidim, and would sit at his spotless table writing scrolls and tefillin and mezuzot, while the other lived in the heart of the town in a draughty shack, pounding with the hammer and striking out sparks of light, and the iron obeyed him doing his will and his desire. I was young and I have grown old, but still the one who sat writing the letters of the Torah, and the other who stood hammering and beating and forging the iron are always in my mind's eye."

His deep love, his devout Jewish faith, the inspiration he absorbed from his beloved Jerusalem, his strong sense of Jewish destiny, his ability to convey the mysticism of the Zohar in his novels, are all combined in his creative works, of unique style unequalled in the world of literature. His crowning recognition was indeed earned when he was invited to Sweden to receive the Nobel prize at the hand of the Swedish monarch.

In his response to the Swedish Academy he said: "In Jerusalem the men of discrimination did not sit down to dine in company until they knew who their companions were to be (Tracte Sanhedrin 23a) so I will now tell you who I am, whom you have agreed to have at your table.

"As a result of the historic catastrophe in which Titus of Rome destroyed Jerusalem and Israel was exiled from its land, I was born in one of the cities of the Exile. But always I regarded myself as one who was born in Jerusalem. In a dream, in a vision of the night, I saw myself standing with my brother Levites in the Holy Temple, singing with them the songs of David, King of Israel, melodies such as no ear has heard since the day our city was destroyed and its people went into exile. I belong to the tribe of Levi; my forebears and I are of the minstrels that were in the Temple, and there is a tradition in my father's family that we are of the lineage of the Prophet Samuel, whose name I bear. I was five years old when I wrote my first song. It was out of longing for my father that I wrote it. It happened that my father, of blessed memory, went away for business. I was overcome for longing for him and I made a song. After I made many songs, but nothing had remained of them all. My father's house, where I left a roomful of writings, was burned down in the First

World War, and all I had left there was burned with it. The young artisans, tailors, and shoe-makers, who used to sing my songs at their work, were killed in the First World War and of those who were not killed in the War, some were buried alive with their sisters in the pits they dug for themselves by the order of the enemy, and most were burned in the crematoria of Auschwitz together with their sisters who had adorned our town with their beauty and sung my songs with their sweet voices. The fate of the singers who, like my songs, went up in flame was also the fate of the books which I later made. All of them went up in flame to Heaven together in a fire which broke out one night in my home in Bad Homburg as I lay ill in a hospital. Among the books which were burned was a large novel of some seven hundred pages, the first part of which the publisher had announced he was about to bring out. . . .

"Who were my mentors in poetry and literature? That is a matter of opinion. Some see in my books the influence of authors whose names in my ignorance I have not even heard, while others see the influences of poets whose names I have heard but whose writings I have not read. And what is my opinion? From whom did I receive nurture? Not every man remembers the name of the cow which supplied him with each drop of milk he has drunk. But in order not to leave you totally in the dark, I will try to clarify from whom I received whatever I have received. There is an influence I have received from every man, every woman, every child I have encountered along my way, both Jews and non-Jews. Peoples' talk and the stories they tell have been engraved on my heart and some of them have come up into my pen. It has been the same way with the spectacles of nature. The Dead Sea, which I used to see every morning at sunrise from the roof of my house, the Arnon Brook in which I used to bathe, the nights I used to spend with devout and pious men at midnight beside the Wailing Wall, nights which gave me eyes to see the Land of the Holy One, Blessed be He, which He gave us, and the city in which He established His name."

Shmuel, who was as devout a vegetarian as he was a Jew, could often be seen shopping and chatting with his friends in Jerusalem. His blue eyes twinkled and his saintly face crowned with white hair, broke into a wry smile as he keenly examined his kasha and gave the shopkeeper his expert opinion. His profound love of nature and his respect for all life may be understood from one of his statements at Stockholm.

"Lest I slight any creature, I must also mention the domestic animals, the beasts and the birds from whom I have learned. Job said long ago (35, 11): 'Who teacheth us more than the beasts of the earth, and maketh us wiser than the fowls of heaven?' Some of what I have learned from them I have written in my books, but I fear that I have not learned as much as I should have done, for when I hear a dog bark, or a bird twitter, or a cock crow, I do not know whether they are thanking me for all I have told of them or calling me to account."

Vegetarians are apt to quote from the unlimited number of eminent vegetarians in all spheres who have graced history to the present day. We are proud that Shmuel Yosef Agnon will rank with the greatest and those who have read his works will know that his writings will inspire future generations as long as the spirit is free to travel in the realms of beauty and imagination.

Milk and Meat
By REV. S. CLAYMAN

The laws about milk and meat play an important part in Jewish diet and in Jewish life. We refrain not only from eating milk and meat together, but even our crockery, cutlery, pots, and pans have to be kept apart.

I remember a strange experience concerning kosher pots and pans during the war when I was Minister to an evacuated congregation in Guilford, Surrey. To begin with most of my congregants after being transported from their bombed-out homes in the East End of London were given temporary bedroom accommodation for the night. They left their bedrooms early in the morning and spent most of their time in a large hall commandeered for their needs. After meals in this hall the evacuees were free to walk the streets of Guilford. In the course of time more satisfactory accommodation was organised for these evacuees.

Two of these families were given a house to share between them. Trouble began with the sharing of one kitchen. The mother of one family was strictly kosher and did not trust any member of the other family. Whenever she left a pan on the stove she tied the lid with string so that trefah food could not accidentally fall or perhaps be deliberately thrown into her kosher pan. Not satisfied with these precautions she appointed one of her daughters to sit or stand closely by the stove to watch. The suspicion between the two families led to friction, and the friction developed into quarrels. I was sent by the officials of the council to make peace.

To the non-Jewish staff of the council the contretemps must have seemed ridiculous. The Kashrut of the one party must have seemed a religion of pots and pans. The whole affair seemed to raise the question "Why all this fuss about milk and meat?"

Before we attempt to find an answer it has to be stated that milk and meat and the dietary laws in general belong to a class of laws which have to be obeyed without questioning. Such laws are called Chukim, and a word has to be said about Chukim.

Whenever a reason is given for any commandment in the Torah there is that human weakness to find an excuse for not observing it. Our duty therefore is to accept and observe the dietary laws, and only to strengthen our observance may we search for the reason.

It is therefore not unreasonable to suppose that the laws of milk and meat which are part of the Jewish dietary system have the motive —the suffering of animals to avoid needless pain to living creatures. To begin with the possibility may seem remote. What has milk and meat (milchik and fleishik) to do with cruelty and kindness towards living creatures?

There is a chapter in the Talmud which deals with this subject. It begins with the words "It is forbidden to cook any kind of meat in milk." We are not taken any further in our enquiry. Meat is already dead and milk is not alive so that cruelty or kindness to animals seems irrelevant to the discussion.

But consider the biblical origin of the prohibition. There it is stated "You shall not cook a kid in its mother's milk." The expression occurs three times in the Pentateuch, once to prohibit the cooking, once to prohibit the eating, and once to prohibit any gain or profit from such cooking. But what a contrast between the emotional words of this expression in the Torah, and the words "milk and meat." The contrast is all the more striking when you read in the Aramaic translation, "You shall not cook meat and milk." This is not the translation at all but a paraphrase.

Take the word גדי (a kid). All Jewish commentators agree that the word applies equally to a calf, to a lamb, or to a young goat. What determines the biblical use of this particular word is that the animal is young.

It is forbidden — as the Talmud teaches us — to boil any meat in milk, and yet the Torah uses three times the word "a kid." There must be some special significance in a word used deliberately, and I believe we can guess what that significance is.

Whatever is young appeals to our emotions, to our sympathy, to our compassion, and to our love. Whether it be a baby, a kitten, a puppy, it evokes such emotions. That seems almost certainly to be the motive for the use of the words *a kid* three times.

Now, let us consider another word אמו (its mother). Why its mother? We are not allowed to cook meat in the milk of any mother. Can anybody deny that the word mother even by itself stirs our compassion. The relationship of a mother to a baby, but especially to its own baby, is something special, unique, and sacred. There is a bond of love which binds them together.

Lastly there is the word חלב (milk). In our context the use of this word has a similar significance. The milk is formed from the body of the mother. It symbolises its readiness to give of its own body, of its very life, its readiness to make any sacrifice for the sake of its baby.

New let me relate an incident which has left an impression on me. It must be about twenty years ago since I visited a museum in Livingstone, Rhodesia. There I saw a number of stuffed animals in a glass cage. One of them was the mother, the others were its young. Underneath the case was typed the story about these animals as follows:

A few travelers came across them — they were alive at the time — in the bush of Africa. A team of wild dogs attacked these animals; wild dogs are very vicious. They bit a hole into the mother's body, but she remained at her post, her body over her young, protecting them to the last. The travelers beat the dogs with heavy sticks and eventually succeeded in driving them away. But they were too late to save these bush animals, which were then donated to the museum, and placed in a glass case as a testimony to the relationship between a mother and its young.

Is It Kosher?

EDITORIAL

Of all the problems brought about by the ingenuity of the human mind, the ability to distort, to adapt and to deflect the written word is perhaps the greatest single challenge which faces legislators in all civilised countries. Whilst this adaptability may afford a measure of relief against oppressive legislation, the conscientious lawmaker who drafts his Bill with the well-being of Society in mind, must suffer torment of the spirit when visualising his carefully worded enactments being scrutinised by myriad volatile minds, all intent on avoiding the provisions, and determined to nullify the effects by protraction evasion and misinterpretation.

Little wonder that the Law given on Mount Sinai was handed down orally from generation to generation in order to preserve its original intentions. Then as now many an astute mind must have sought a way to lessen personal responsibility, whilst desiring to live in respectable conformity. But with the dispersion, the scribes with loving care wrote down the enactments, so that in the wanderings the words of the Torah should not be for ever lost.

The battalions of erstwhile slaves were morally incapable of immediate return to the natural state of pre-Noah ancestry; to lust on flesh was acceded as an inherited barbaric practice, and the laws of compassion formed the first stepping stone in the long trek toward the Messianic era. Thus the precepts, elementary and unambiguous, were ordained, and in the laws relating to Kasruth certain basic principles cannot be ignored.

In the Mosaic era the boundaries of cruelty and disease were simply though effectively defined, and the provisions made were adequate for the circumstances. The Sabbath Day was granted to all and Rashi comments that even domestic creatures at least on that day, must not be enclosed but shall be free to graze and enjoy the work of creation. If now they are incarcerated in darkened containers seven days and seven nights in each week for the entire period of their lives; if they neither see the luminaries of the heavens nor experience the sweet smell and the taste of the pastures, has not the most sacred Sabbath Law been flagrantly violated and can the flesh of their bodies be Kosher?

Would the law that states "Thou shalt not muzzle the ox when he treads the corn" acquiesce in the computerised feeding of chemical fatteners, whilst the poor beast scents the dew and clover in the meadows beyond his darkened cell?

When it is written "Thou shalt not yoke an ox with an ass," does it imply that a calf may spend its entire life standing on slats, never to lie down, and effectively chained to the sides by its neck to prevent it doing so? Is this a perversion of the Torah? And when the unfortunate victim is slaughtered can its remains be Kosher?

If the law forbids one to cause distress to a mother bird by removing eggs from the nest in her presence, would it concur that during its lifetime a hen could be shut up in a receptacle of twelve square inches, its beak removed and feathers clipped? And after its throat is cut, would its body be Kosher for food?

If a cruelly treated animal shall be considered unfit for food, and if the measure of the cruelty is determined by its ability to walk, do the authorities inspect the incarcerated animals in the factory farms, and is there any record as to whether they are able to walk to their own slaughter on their own emaciated legs? And if not is their flesh Kosher?

If, apart from the humane aspects, the method of killing shows concern for the avoidance of the disease and plague which stems from bloodstreams linked with our own, would not the law be interpreted to reject cattle whose bodies are heavily impregnated with dangerous antibiotics? And if these antibiotics cannot be eliminated when the flesh pots are heated, and if many human deaths result from their intake, and if the most conservative of all learned societies, the British Medical Association, has declared the danger and asked for restrictive legislation, would it be reasonable to assume that the Torah is being thwarted and would such flesh be considered Kosher? And even if it were not so considered, would it be forbidden as a possible danger to life(Tractate Avodah Sorah 30A.)

If the law forbids the mixing of species, even of plants, and confusion of sexes, would it condone the injection of female hormones into the male beast, even though it is acknowledged to be cancerous in practice? And when this distortion of blood is covered with earth, even as is human blood, is this respect for the Creator who saw that all he created was very good? Or is this confusion, is it defilement, is it sacrilege, and is the flesh still Kosher?

Are the authorities aware that in Great Britain, as in most countries, over eighty percent of the animals slaughtered are from factory farms, and contrary to the intentions of the Torah, are reared with total lack of compassion, bearing the seed of malignant disease, threatening the carnivore with disastrous consequences, and under-mining the ordinances protecting man from the folly of self-annihilation?

Shall the devout continue to desecrate the Sabbath Day by placing the corpse of such a bird or beast in front of the Sabbath lights in memory of the creation? And shall those rays of light which for thousands of years symbolised the search for truth and knowledge, be now perverted to illuminate apathy, dishonesty, and ignorance?

Shall a certificate of Beth Din convey that Torah min hasha-mayim has been sincerely observed, or shall it become a licence for misinterpretation, evasion, and permission to the beholder to bow down each man to the God of his own stomach?

And when will the womenfolk cease to cry out for permission to eat the backsides of animals and instead clamour for an investigation as to whether the evils of factory farms are making a mockery of their Kashruth?

Let all who are observant and devout remember that the responsibility is their own, no Jew can use an intermediary, whether in this case it be a Beth Din, a Board of Shechita, or just a Kosher butcher with a label on his window. If unaware of the facts, his is a sin of omission, if he is aware and chooses to ignore his personal responsibility, his is a sin of commission; he is eating Trefah. The Torah must not be brought into disrepute. The ways of the batteries and factory farms are not the ways of pleasantness, and no distortion of underlying principles can give validity to a signed certificate or grant absolution to the conscience of the individual.

Let us be quite clear, these comments are not questioning the Law, neither is any reflection intended on the sincere and learned leaders. It is a quest for knowledge and understanding in an age which has brought the living atom into our daily lives and with it a confusion of accepted principles. Neither is this a dissertation on methods of slaughter; we oppose the immoral practice of breeding and rearing living beings for food and we are not concerned with a discussion on the niceties of this or that method of killing. We oppose the entire concept of feeding on our fellow creatures: it is an abomination. The questions have been asked and the replies are now sought. We seek true and sincere statements based on the principles of the Torah and shall continue to ask these questions until the answer is forthcoming.

Bring Back The Sabbatical

EDITORIAL

Before the world proliferation of motor vehicles, the Bank of England crossroads in the City of London was the busiest spot on earth. Clustered around the great building with the nation's gold stored deep under the River Thames, are the head offices of many banks and insurance institutions, the Mansion House where the Lord Mayor resides, and the imposing Royal Exchange, where for generations the world's basic commodities changed hands. On these broad approach steps visitors retreat, to gaze at the equerries commissionnaires, stock exchange runners, and others (some in their ancient city garb), and the never-ending flow of red buses and other traffic interchanging in every direction.

Few turn about and gaze upwards to the great portico with the central motif representing commerce, and surrounded by figures of Hindu, Greek, Armenian, Turkish, Negro, and other traders bringing their produce to the City Exchange. Or to the plinth of the building with the words engraved thereon "The Earth is the Lord's and the fullness thereof." Those who do rarely comprehend that in these few trite words lies the solution to many of the basic economic ills that bedevil the twentieth century.

The acceptance of this principle implies acceptance of the Sabbatical Year. "Six years thou shalt sow thy field, and six years thou shalt prune thy vineyard, and gather in the produce thereof. But the seventh year shall be a Sabbath of solemn rest for the land. . . thou shalt neither sow thy field, nor prune thy vineyard."

Each seventh year which we have been able to reach by some miraculous means, is the Sabbatical Year. This is the year in which the land itself has been granted one year's complete rest without let or hindrance. This is the inalienable and unalterable condition of occupation, implacable in its operation and ignored by humanity at their peril.

Few have the courage to accept the biblical declaration that the earth does not belong to the children of men and that they have no automatic or absolute right to possession of the earth's surface or indeed to the benefits deriving therefrom. We turn aside from this command as if it did not exist; we avoid examining the ancient legal document that contains the clauses and defines the conditions under which we are granted leasehold rights to occupy and work this earthly domain. We hope that by long usage of squatters' rights, some of the more onerous conditions in the agreement will have gone by default, or perhaps that the Landlord (whom we are inclined to believe is an absentee one), may by now have forgotten to enforce the clauses; or has become disinterested in the present occupants and cannot be bothered to refer to the original terms. In long leases, misuse, neglect of maintenance, and failure to observe basic conditions, is not unusual, unless compulsively enforced.

The granting of this rest produces a twofold benefit. In the fallow year the land regains its fertility and continues in productiveness; the tiller of the soil free from his physical labour, his time devoted to spiritual development and mental studies, returns rejuvenated in mind, spirit and body to the land again fertile, and eager for the application of a further six years' husbandry.

Technicians and wranglers, expert in the mathematics of agriculture, horticulture, silviculture, agronomy, zoology, ecology, and the rest, emboldened with authority they have been able to scrape together from the collected theories left to them, have declared that a fallow year is not possible in a modern state; the economy would suffer and irrepairable damage would be done to the land and its environs.

Now anyone who has tilled the land or kept a garden, and has not been brainwashed with chemical fertilizers, insecticides, and pesticides; anyone who does not go into fits of depression on seeing a sprouting weed or give way to violent homicidal instincts when spying a centipede making its innocent way to its habitation, or go livid with greed at the sight of a bird pecking away at the best apple on the tree; such a person will have experienced the almost unlimited yield that the peaceful use and the granting of rest will provide from the land under his care. There will be more than sufficient for his needs, for the beasts and birds and indeed even the insects, all of whom will share the copious bounty provided, not only during the year of rest but in the extra productiveness of the land in the remaining six years. Every harvest, hundreds of thousands of tons of produce are destroyed by the agricultural countries; tomatoes, bananas, apples, pears, peaches, wheat, and many other products, and from the European Community we perforce receive payment of one hundred pounds sterling an acre to terminate surplus production.

Shemita, as the Sabbatical Year is known, is entirely in accord with the vegetarian philosophy of the Bible. In fact it is only under a vegetarian economy, at least for the sixth and seventh year, that the observance of this great principle could be carried out. "Six years thou shalt sow thy land, and gather in the increase thereof, but the seventh year thou shalt let it rest and lie fallow, that the poor of thy people may eat; and what they leave the beast of the field shall eat. In like manner thou shalt deal with thy vineyard and with thy oliveyard."

It does not provide for shiploads of fodder to be removed from the land and exported to feed factory farm birds and beasts incarcerated in the gluttonous domains of U.S.A., Britain, France, Germany, and the rest. The wastages would be too great, over ninety percent of this produce is lost in conversion to flesh, and the undernourished people in the grain growing countries would suffer still further by the denial of the Sabbath produce of their land. Indeed the present system of factory farming would not be possible if the Sabbatical were recognized. Even in recent dock strikes massive stocks of imported "feed" (which at all times places a heavy strain on balance of payments) ran so low after two weeks that a great slaughter of animal-kind was planned in case the strike continued. The land cannot support human flesh-eaters!

What staggering changes would occur if Shemita were observed. What would the Boards of Shechita do without the multifarious quarrels of the slaughterers demanding higher prices for the cruel and dirty work they carry out on behalf of the community. What an opportunity would arise in the great realm of Jewish spiritual understanding, when the people's main interest would cease to be the eating or not eating of animal's backsides. What a vista of idealism would open up for the youth of today who are striving to make their meaningless lives worthwhile again. And where would Blooms be with their saltpetered slabs of flesh; and Frohwein's with their van-loads of Belsen looking chickens, and Skreks whose pieces of animal are canned up enabling the uric-acid to multiply before eaten. What hysteria in the packing yards of Chicago and the infested killing grounds of the Argentine! The Shemita year would bring all this fiendish activity to a stop; the breeding and the bleeding, the bludgeoning and killing and the vending of corpses!

And what of the drug companies, where would they be if the population took to a more natural and harmonious way of living? And the surgeons with their enlarged fees, facing a dearth of human organs infected by the intake of animal diseases and requiring removal. Then there is the building industry engaged in great hospital and vivisection building programmes; they would have to turn aside and build homes for the people. Good Lord what a change in the economy when all these trades would have to seek a more kindly and helpful means of creating profits.

Perhaps the Sabbatical Year is the answer after all!

The Gentle Art Of Walking

EDITORIAL

It is indeed a sign of the times to refer to walking as a gentle art considering that it is as primaeval and basic as breathing or eating.

Nevertheless numberless persons spend much of their time and money in seeking health and pleasure but succeed only in losing both.

Yet the vast numbers that comprise the armchair suicide squad who move awkwardly from bed to car to office desk, to car to telly seat and finally to bed again, forget that both enjoyment and health are to be had for the asking. One might say that it is almost impossible to be ill if one walks sufficiently, but today this has become a lost art and needs to be restudied.

When the sun is rising in the Eastern sky, the song birds fill the sweet and as yet unpolluted air, and the dew sparkles like a million diamonds balanced on the top of each tiny blade of grass, it is then that one should feel the urge to get away from the fume-filled shopping streets and the motorway madness. We have the finest Ordinance Survey in the world—throughout the land every cottage every clump of trees, every footpath, every farmgate is clearly and accurately shown on the map together with every rise and fall of the surface. What greater adventure than to decide to explore a little or much of the beautiful land in which we live by the most natural means available—the legs that God has given us.

Firstly then to buy a map of the proposed area—a one-inch scale and a small hand compass to protect against the almost impossible eventuality of getting lost, a small (very small) haversack, as it is not proposed to take the kitchen sink with; or to travel like a laden donkey. Greatest consideration should be given to the avoidance of weight, and the clothing to be worn should be of the lightest, together with the minimum of toilet requirements. No change of wearing apparel, if necessary a small article could be purchased en route. No food (except perhaps one apple), one does not need to be stuffing that hole in the head all the time, and a tiny village shop is always near. The object of the haversack is to carry a super lightweight plastic mac and a thin wind-cheater. Even the weight of the map should be reduced by cutting it to leave only the immediate requirements of the route. Under no circumstances should a timepiece or camera be taken so that the vacation should be as light and free as the spring air.

No detailed timetable should be prepared lest it interfere with the freedom of action, but the map can be marked to show which of the many lovely little old-world villages en route could be a possible stopping point. Most of the villages and hamlets have an ancient inn in which charming night accommodation is available. Low ceilinged, sloping floored rooms where King Charles II fled from his enemies, or Cromwell stopped the night; and where a new form of education can be acquired by listening to the sound, salty, down-to-earth conversations of the locals, until one realizes that the strength of a country is embodied in its country-folk.

Now anyone who can walk for ten minutes, whether he be aged eight or eighty, can embark on this self-propelled voyage with safety and great enjoyment—the distances can be adjusted accordingly. Take a public service vehicle to beyond the urban area and let the first day's travel be low, whether it be two or ten miles in order to limber up the strength of the atrophied muscles of the legs. Next day one will want to exceed the first, and thereafter the sheer joy of walking will make the decision to stop a difficult one.

Take a route in a Southerly direction so that one will be walking into the sun, which gives a tremendous lift to the spirit, and let the destination be a place you love or where you have always wanted to visit. If the sun be hot (and it is surprising how often it is in the countryside) find a sheltered corner and snooze in the early afternoon, on the cut grass or a pile of hay, retire early and arise with the awakening morn.

How fortunate we are that here all footpaths are clearly sign-posted. What a thrill to anticipate the next item on the map, a farm, a cottage or a stream, and as the beautiful panorama changes as one steps along, the legend on the map comes to life exactly as marked. On the tiny lanes or footpaths away from the mainstream of life, the great trees in all their magnificent variety extend a gracious welcome whilst the tiny wild flowers smile up with their rare and winsome beauty. A pheasant darts out from the hedgerows showing its strength and beauty; little white bob-tails disappear into the braken or a tiny black lamb will run to the edge of its enclosure trying to say "Hello friend, lovely to see you."

The footpaths will run by brookside and over hillocks, hard by ancient and forgotten manors, over tiny bridges and remote railway lines long since closed. When emerging into some historic village with its inhabitants going about their village life it will be as if a long-lost community has been rediscovered, and when the thrilling journey ends, be it twenty or 200 miles, the pilgrim will be uplifted in spirit, fit in physique, reaffirmed with a deep and abiding faith, and a heart full of gratitude for the beneficence that has enabled him to know the loveliness of the world in which he lives.

The Lost Hyphen
EDITORIAL

With the approach of the summer months, people of all ages turn seriously to thoughts of holidays in the sun "away from it all." Visions come to mind of a turquoise sea gently lapping the golden sands of a tree-lined lagoon, or perhaps the breath-taking view of distant mountain peaks seen from the balcony of a chalet nestling among the pines. Howbeit, fancy turns to reality and at the appropriate time the great trek commences; each hour fifty thousand cars disgorge themselves from London and proportionately from other centres. The roads to the coast and the ferry boats are jammed with frustrated and anxious human freight. Harrassed dock-side officials are ever anxious to help move this continuous living column over to other shores, there to sort itself out on the greater land mass. Once released on to the sun-drenched, blood-bespattered roads of France, Spain, and Italy, the real vacation begins. A thousand miles of nerve-racking driving by a thousand nerve-racked drivers going in both directions in hostile mutuality, happily unaware of the peaceful villages that lie within the sound of their motor-horns. As the sun beats down mercilessly, the overheated, overcramped occupants fight heroically to deny themselves the natural blessing of sleep. The nightmare, like all nightmares, eventually comes to an end, and our travellers, tense and with tempers frayed, arrive in a state of semi-collapse. The awakening brings happier anticipation as the blue sea, cliffs, and Meditteranean pines become a reality.

In the multistoried monstrosity, which in the present state of understanding provides what is known as a luxury hotel, a variety of indigestible and often dangerous comestibles, in quantities three or four times the amount needed, will be provided. In the main this will consist of creatures which in their dead state have been temporarily suspended in their process of putrifaction by means of refrigeration. Aided by the climate, this putrifaction, however, will proceed at a greatly accelerated pace between refrigeration and table. Often there will be new and unknown Mediterranean creatures, prepared in new and unknown ways the better to entice carnivorous appetites to take in a larger quantity of these victuals than the recipients' stomachs, hearts, livers, kidneys, etc. can possibly cope with. In the evening the cacophony of a discordant band will provide ample background noise for the animated conversation that results when meeting one's friends and associates from back home. This is an excellent opportunity to discuss business, tax matters, and domestic problems resulting in the hotel really becoming "home from home."

Comes the happy day to return, when the procedures of the outward journey are reversed. Our vacationists will arrive back, please God, to the comfort of their homes, nervously and physically exhausted and in a state of spiritual bankruptcy.

The holiday slides will be shown to a gathering of friends in the centrally heated room with cigarette smoke cosily filling the atmosphere. Accompanied by the social practice of eating beef sandwiches, preserved in saltpetre as another means of stopping putrefaction, the slides of the happy summer days will be thrown on the screen as an additional, if not equal, attraction to the ever present "mechia" of the television.

The Baal Shem Tov attained his spiritual heights in the solitude of the fields and forests where far away from the distraction of humankind he could meditate upon the great manifestations of life of which we are such a minute but integral part. Long before the era of national holidays, the Jewish Sabbath and festivals laid down a pattern of leisure which calmed the spirit and brought back purpose into our lives, and regained for us a sense of proportion.

Today one may still spend one's vacation rising in the morning to the sound of a whispering breeze as the earth joyously awakes; one may still wander by lonely sea coasts where only the waves coming home to rest tell of their journey across the seven seas. As ever before one may still traverse the mountain heights and the silent woods and listen to the heart of God beating in the trees. True, it means departing for a time from one's car and regaining the use of the atrophied muscles of one's legs, but there are few, even the ailing, who cannot eventually achieve this with advantage. Certainly it means the simple life with natural food and perhaps a couple of days semi-fasting to fit one for this great experience. Undoubtedly one must give up predatory habits to avoid leaving a trail of blood and suffering in one's wake; there must be a time of peace and harmony in order to understand the miracle of the tiniest alpine flower and the unity of many different creatures following their uninterrupted lives. "In quietness and confidence shall be your strength." Let re-creation not recreation be the aim in your choice of future vacations.

Chad Gadyu

It is strange to think that for thousands of years children have been sitting down to Seder with their parents singing the ancient melodies, being inspired by the story of how Moses turned a despairing collection of slaves into a disciplined nation. The Passover proclaims a stirring message for freedom and equality both for the home-born and the stranger alike. It condemns slavery not only of the person but also slavery of the spirit.

As the melody lingers on into the night I wonder how many are awake when everyone joins in the final chorus of Chad Gadyu, or will be dozing and suddenly awake with the rousing notes of the first verse?

Chad Gadyu is a very jolly way to finish the Seder, but why it was included in the service and why the place of honour given to it at the end, unlike the solemn rendering of Yigdol or Adon Olum with which the Synagogue services finish? After all it is just a fanciful rhyme like the house that Jack built. Or is it? Not really, because Chad Gadyu has a very deep and important lesson for all humanity to learn, a lesson that perhaps very few are aware of.

"One only kid which my father bought—and a cat came and devoured the kid." Here is the first act of cruelty and destruction. Each act of killing must bring retribution, thus one crime produces another. "The dog came," and "The stick came" and the fire and the water and the ox and the slaughter. Finally the chain of retribution is stopped by the destruction of the Angel of Death. The moral is that only God who gives life can take it away and whether it be human or animal, man has no right or power to do so and if he does, retribution sets in. All know the story of Noah ". . .when the earth was filled with violence" and finally God stopped it with the flood. Jewish teachings clearly tell us that we have not the right to kill whether it be fellow man or our younger fellow creatures and if we do we bring on further bloodshed. This is precisely what is happening in the world today. Wars will never cease so long as we have no mercy on the little creatures who cannot plead for themselves and who have such love for us. To kill them and eat them of course is unforgivable, so next time when all sing Chad Gadyu let the real meaning prevail that it is against God's intention for us to bring violence into the world; to cry out for the fleshpots of Egypt when we have been given manna to eat. If all refuse to eat the flesh of creatures that have been killed, we shall be able to reverse the song of Chad Gadyu and finish at the beginning, with the kid "that my father bought for two zuzzim" being alive and happy and loved by everyone.

May we all sing Chad Gadyu next year in Jerusalem.

Let It Be!

EDITORIAL

"I know a bank where the wild thyme blows,
Where oxlips and the nodding violet grows,
Quite overcanopied with luscious woodbine,
With sweet musk roses, and with eglantine."
'A Midsummer Night's Dream'

Slowly, all too slowly, in this Northern clime, the dreams of warm sunny days give way reluctantly to realization.

The magic of midsummer ever beckons to the land where seabirds call, to where hurrying waves seek their rest on the golden pebbled beach; to the serenity of mountain heights, and to sleepy valleys cradled amid the hills in peaceful soliloquy.

Maybe disillusionment is around the corner, but in the country of the mind, distance does not weary nor disappointment mar the adventure of enchanted summer hours.

But the drowsy heat of noon or the evening zephyr gently blowing cannot easily dispel the pressing impact of realities, unless a firm decision be taken to avoid the ever lurking scowl of the monster.

The first step to escape for a while from the trials and tribulations of everyday existence, is to disconnect entirely from the endless dirge of the news media. Times were when only local tragedies were reported, but with technical wherewithal, worldwide misfortunes now garnered speedily, are added to forebodings of doom and disseminated in repeated doses, until discord, depression, and dismay have been established in full measure.

After all, murders, muggings, and maulings, fraud, famine, and fighting, perfidy, double talk and much else, too, have been with us ever since the epoch-shaking discovery of the flint axe-head.

But such happenings form only a minute part of the world scene; unrecorded are the voluminious acts of human kindness and earnest endeavour. Therefore let peace reign for a while; shun the newspapers and the posters, disconnect the television and silence the boring ballyhoo of the radio.

With this achieved, faith in human nature will return, and the joy of summer will break through the cloud of despond that encircles the earth.

Switch off, too, from the disturbing trivialities of everyday life, senseless jealousies, tiresome neighbours, the unkept-appointments and badly executed work, builders resting on the job awaiting their pension day, and traders engaged in the time-honoured custom of petty overcharging. Cast aside the daily slavery of the cooker and the sink. At no time did God command that the food he provided shall be baked, boiled, grilled, and ground; neither are children (or adults if it comes to that) empty sacks that have to be filled up at least three times a day.

Emerge for a while from the news-polluted ether and the slavery of acquired habits; draw a great magic circle wherein the song of birds and the whispering breeze gently release the spirit, and open the eyes to reveal a world of entrancing beauty and perfection.

Search out a place far from the madding crowd, where the hotline from the office cannot reach and the raucus cacophony of the discotheque is not. Where the clattering cleverness of the jabber-wocks from back home is somewhere else; where over-precocious offspring are not heard and success-sodden stories cannot be purveyed.

True it will all be waiting still; noxious exhaust fumes and wail of ambulances; the unheard cries of creatures in darkened cells and their silent, patient, unending tread to the hidden horrors of the abattoirs. The cellophane wrapped flesh packs will still be on sale in the supermarkets, and the vultures will still pick flesh from the bones of the dying and the dead.

But within the magic circle, behind the glistening moat, the drawbridge shall be lowered and the ascent made to the highest turret of the ivory tower, from whence the petty tittle-tat of talebearing of the self-sufficient and the woebegone wail of hypo-chondriachs shall fade away into the silence.

The sunkissed honeysuckled path shall wind its pleasant way to the horizon: only the laughter of little children, the bleating of a lamb or the distant barking of a dog, shall disturb the cloud-lightened footsteps, stepping onward toward the place where heaven's harmony descends on the sunbeams; where unseen messengers traversing the molecular paths of the universe bring a harvest of health and well-being. Here then to dwell with the tall trees reaching upwards and clad in their green garments of majesty; to join them in their silent Amidah prayer. Here to participate in the Hallelujah chorus of the multitudinous flowers, singing in their great festival of praise to the Creator.

Let it be! Even though for a brief summer trance. Let reality go, until the festival of summer shall pass. Refreshed from the cosmic stream of life, let autumn be joined with grateful decision to contribute, each according to his ability and opportunity, to the universal need; to the cause of the weak and the oppressed, the misused and the unprotected. Each his allotted share toward evolutionary adjustment and advancement until the millenium be achieved.

After all, is not this what life is all about?

Tu Bi Shevat

A Happy New Year to all trees!

Why is the festival of New Year for the Trees celebrated on the fifteenth of Shevat? It is because most of the annual rain in Israel falls before that date and thereafter the sap begins to fill the trees and their lives are renewed for another year of blossom and fruit. The "Shekadiah"—the almond tree, is the herald of Spring and it has pride of place in the celebration, for its rosy white buds are the first to blossom even before its leaves have sprouted. On this day the "tithe" was reckoned, and Jewish farmers were obliged to take a tenth of their new fruit and crop produce to the Temple in Jerusalem.

In ancient times it was a custom to plant a cedar sapling on the birth of a boy, and a cypress sapling on the birth of a girl. The cedar symbolised strength and stature of man while the cypress signified the fragrance and gentleness of woman. When the children were old enough, it was their task to care for the trees which had been planted in their honour. Today the main celebrations on Tu B'Shevat is the tree planting ceremony, when pupils from every school assemble and follow their teachers into the countryside to plant young saplings. It makes the children aware of the need for re-afforestation and soil conservation to beautify the country.

In the Bible there are many lovely references to trees:

"For you shall go out with joy, and be led forth in peace; The mountains and the hills before you shall break forth into singing. And all the trees of the field shall clap their hands. Instead of the thorn shall come up the cypress. Instead of the briar shall come up the myrtle." (Isaiah 55.)

"They shall sit every man under his vine and under his fig-tree." (Micah 4.)

"Let the field exult, and everything in it. Then shall all the trees of the wood sing for joy." (Psalms 96.)

"For the Lord thy God brings you into a good land, a land of brooks, of water, of fountains and springs flourishing forth in valleys and hills, a land of wheat and barley, and vines and fig-trees and promegranates; a land of olive trees and honey." (Deut. 8.)

There is also a great deal in the Talmud on the care and love that should be showed toward trees because at the beginning of Creation it is written "And God planted the Garden of Eden." Here are a few extracts.

"You shall not say: 'We shall dwell and not concern ourselves with planting,' but as others planted for you, so shall you plant for your children."

"Once while Choni Hame'agel was walking along a road he saw a man planting a carob tree. Choni asked him: 'How many years will it require for this tree to give forth fruit?' The man answered, that it would require seventy years. Choni asked, 'Are you so hale a man that you expect to live that length of time and eat of its fruit?' The man answered, 'I found a fruitful world because my forefathers planted for me. So will I do the same for my children.' "

"The tender roots of the fig split the hard rock of the crag."

"The palm tree casts its shadow far from itself. The palm tree has no blemish. It provides dates for food, lullavim (branches) for Succot prayers, foliage for the Succah, fibres for ropes, leaves for winnowing purposes, and beams for supporting the ceilings and roof of the house."

"It is forbidden to dwell in a city that has no garden in it."

This beautiful prayer is said at the tree-planting ceremony.

Give dew for a blessing
And cause beneficient rains to fall in their season
To satiate the mountains of Israel and her valleys

And to water thereon every plant and tree
And these saplings
Which we plant before thee this day.
Make deep their roots and wide their crown
That they may blossom forth in grace
Amongst all the trees of Israel
For good and for beauty.

ʿThe Sephardis have their own form of service which is printed in a small book called "Pri Etz Hadar" (Fruit of Goodly Trees) and a section of it comprises seventeen short chapters, each dealing with a different type of fruit grown in the Holy Land. At the conclusion of the reading of each of these chapters, the particular fruit described therein is eaten, and it is accompanied with four glasses of wine, one at the reading of each appropriate passage. No mention is made however, as to the maximum size of the glasses!

Shakespeare's Early Life

Butcher, Tanner, or Teacher?

There was poverty and social difficulty in John Shakespeare's household and the boy early succeeded to his father's trade. This trade is known to have had some connection with the slaughter of animals but it is not thought to be butchery.

On the other hand, a glover, dealing in wool and hides may very well have tapped the stream of supply higher up by conducting a slaughterhouse of his own. Were there such premises adjacent? William could have known all about the horrid exercise and may have been, no doubt reluctantly, an assistant in the dispatch of animals. That he gloated rhetorically over the demise of a calf seems extremely unlikely in the case of one so sensitive to the suffering of animals hunted or otherwise attacked.

It is worth noting that Shakespeare drew a number of metaphors from the butcher's craft, especially in the earlier plays. Dr. Caroline Spurgeon in *Shakespeare's Imagery* observes: In 2 and 3 Henry VI, outside the symbol of the fruit and flower garden, already noticed, there is the even more obvious one of the butcher and the slaughter house, slightly carried on in Richard III. King Henry's compassion for the doomed Duke of Gloucester is thus expressed:

And as the butcher takes away the calf,
And binds the wretch, and beats it when it strays,
Nearing it to the bloody slaughter house;

Even so remorselessly have they borne him hence:
And as the dam runs lowing up and down,
Looking the way her harmless young one went,
And can do naught but wail her darling's loss;
Even so myself bewails good Gloster's case
With sad unhelpful tears; and with dimmed eyes
Look after him and cannot do him good —
So mighty are his avowed enemies."

A little later the Earl of Warwick is back in the metaphorical shambles, though such aristocrats would hardly draw their similes from the common trade of the flesher.

Who finds the heifer dead and bleeding fresh,
And sees just by a butcher with an axe
But will suspect 'twas he that made the slaughter.

The third part of Henry VI intensifies the talk of knives and butchers, as Dr. Spurgeon reminds us:

In 3 Henry VI, Clifford, Edward and Clarence are all called "Butchers", Richard is "that devil's butcher", Parliament is thought of as a "shambles" and the realm as a "slaughter house". Gloucester sees himself hewing his way to the crown with a bloody axe and Henry, when Gloucester comes to kill him, pictures himself very aptly as a sheep yielding his throat to the butcher's knife."

The fact that Shakespeare knew something of the shambles craft which drew its material from the slaughterhouse does not prove that he was participating or even a worker definitely apprenticed therein. (He may have given an occasional hand or he may have written of what he saw, not of what he practised.) It is obvious that a boy so receptive to the beauty of things would rather be away from the blood and guts, the squalor and suffering of the butcher's yard. Whither would he turn? To another trade or to school teaching, later suggestions have favoured the last.

Later the intricate social pattern of the Middle Ages was broken up by the Rennaissance, which let in a new classical art and the

Reformation which let in the new religion. The Elizabethans were living in a fresh light with a great darkness separating them from the old light. The famous and forward-looking speech of prophecy and blessing delivered by Cranmer over "this royal infant," Elizabeth in Henry VIII reflected this new atmosphere.

> In her days every man shall eat in safety
> Wonder his own vine what he plants and sing
> The merry songs of peace to all his neighbours."

It is evident that any compulsive connection that Shakespeare may have experienced in his early days with butchery or the trades connected therewith produced in him only compassion which often appeared in his writings during later life.

What Is Jewish About Vegetarianism?

EDITORIAL

Like the little slave girl Topsy in *Uncle Tom's Cabin*, who when asked about her parents, replied, "I didn't have any, I just growed," so some of the world's finest institutions (one example is the British Constitution) just grow as the circumstances compel. And because they grow, which is Nature's way, they are very real and purposeful, filling the need which brought them into existence.

The Jewish Vegetarian Movement comes within this category, but to satisfy the inquisitive it is necessary to explain its philosophy, and achievements.

All people who are conscious of the cruelty and obscenity of carnivorism have a duty to help in accordance with their ability. The fulfilment of the simple command "Thou shalt not kill" is the basis of vegetarianism and in its elementary stage asks no more and no less from those adopting this way of life. To change a person's habitual diet is to change the person himself and this deals out a rather nasty blow to the ego. Therefore ask no more but that the individual shall continue his customary life in all its spheres whilst replacing the habit of feeding on flesh with the many happy alternatives available. This is indeed a fair exchange to achieve renunciation of cruelty and disease which are the grim by-products of the butcher's wares.

No need for an international code of vegetarianism implied or expressed; no need to emphasise a particular religion; no need to look to any land for guiding principles; no need to consider learning or intelligence as a condition precedent; no need to indicate the prohibition of one's pet foibles. Even the obvious expectation of good health and prolonged youth is unessential. The doctrine of compassion is basic and elementary and all other adjustments will naturally flow therefrom. After all, even health is a product of many factors, not the least being self-expression and contentment with one's lot.

Therefore let each person be true unto themselves, whether Catholic, Moslem, Jew, Buddhist; let each be proud of their traditions and nationality whether American, Indian, Israeli, Hottentot; let each live and evolve from their own practices even malpractices.

If each retains the best in their inheritance and respects the desire of others to do likewise, would not this be fertile soil in which to plant the seed?

The practice of vegetarianism must in no way be considered as changing the ethnic, spiritual, or even national heritage of the individual, or to impair the enjoyment of inherited ways of life, indigenous cultures thoughts and languages. The great leap forward of the Vegetarian Movement, indicates similar possibilities if other societies existed for other large ethnic groups who could explore this new way of life, and who could feel at home in the uninhibited company and thoughts of their own kith and kin. This is not separatism, it is the most economic use of resources contributing to the common weal.

Of course Jewish people the world over have different eating habits, their peculiar cookery and traditional dishes for festivals have been handed down over the centuries and have almost become a part of their religion. When introducing vegetarianism, therefore, a clear understanding is needed to achieve change or substitutions. Adherence to the Torah and its application to every aspect of Jewish life is as vital today to the average Jew as it was 4,000 years ago, and produces complex questions which call for specialised understanding.

The bond with Israel creates a desire to be in contact with its large vegetarian population; the glorious sunshine, abundant produce and the people's traditional love of the healing arts, provide the ideal setting for a return to natural living. We aim to be of help in the country's long and arduous passage toward fulfilment of the peaceful kingdom so beautifully prophesied by Isaiah.

What is Jewish about vegetarianism? To all people the teachings clearly indicate the compassionate way of life and the prophecy of a return to peace on earth under a beneficent Creator. The lesson of Genesis must needs be retold, "To man and to all creatures have I given a living soul." This is our beginning, mankind and all sentient creatures with a common soul and the earth created for all, not for one species however highly evolved. Until the time of Noah, he who killed a creature was of equal guilt as if he had killed a man: Abel killed an animal, Cain killed Abel, and the chain of retribution has lasted to the present day. Here we arrive at one of the most vital statements in the Bible, a turning point in the history of man, but ignored to provide justification for the continued practice of violence: "I will not again curse the ground anymore for man's sake for the imagination of man's heart is evil from his youth. . .Man was permitted to live in violence—and pay retribution in respect thereof. Why is this rational and awe-inspiring statement ignored? Is the morsel of flesh, the product of suffering and violence, so indispensable that the retribution in human suffering means but little?

Even after entering the land of Israel it was a serious crime to kill an animal and it brought on severe punishment of the law. True, sacrifices were ordained for they knew no other way of worship; to appease gods with the slaughter of children on the altars of stone was customary throughout the known world. Sacrifice is an essential part of the human emotion, but with the progress of centuries it lives on to help the helpless, relieve the oppressed and to fight for justice where none exists. The Laws of Moses built a bulwark against cruelty and inhumanity. It has never been a "Mitzvah" to consume the flesh of creatures and the laws relating to this subject form part of a permissive doctrine only in order to circumscribe the unavoidable cruelties inherent in the carnivorous way of life.

Throughout the ages great Rabbis, Sages, men learned in the arts and sciences, poets and singers of Israel have clearly understood and lived by the Jewish philosophy of compassion.

The Movement has spread and has helped change the climate of opinion. Time was when thrombic carnivores grinned on hearing the word vegetarianism, and with bombast worthy of a better cause, proudly murmured "Meshugga!" Now, the least to be expected is a grudging concurrence.

Many who would not break a twig or switch a light on the Sabbath to avoid interfering with the work of creation, would nevertheless desecrate the Friday night table with the corpse of a creature slaughtered in honour of the Sabbath day. It is "Chillul ha'Shem."

To a people who, throughout thousands of years have contributed more than their share in the sphere of humanitarian causes, and whose reward has often been degradation and physical brutality, may we be forgiven if we suggest, that just for once in a while we enjoy the satisfaction of working through the inspiration of our own teachings, of seeing the results of that work, and of helping towards the fulfilment of the prophecy that Israel shall be a blessing unto the nations.

Let those who ask "What is Jewish about vegetarianism?" ponder on the above and seek clarification. The simple answer is because so many Jewish people are responding to the Movement and becoming vegetarian.

The Enemy Within

EDITORIAL

*"When thou shalt eat the labour of thy hands, happy shalt thou
be, and it shall be well with thee"—Psalms.*

In a broadcast interview, Golda Meir, Prime Minister of Israel, was
asked to give her opinion of Moses. Her humorous reply was "What
should my opinion be? He led us for forty years in a wilderness
and eventually brought us to the one spot in the Middle East where
there was no oil!"

Perhaps this was one reason why the journey took forty years! It
is not an easy task to find a spot in the Middle East that is devoid
of oil, but Moses found it, and thus his people have been spared the
demoralizing effects that result from unearned prosperity. The promise
was, that at the end of this, the longest trek in history, there would
be a land flowing with milk and honey, not with mineral oil and
gold deposits. A land where the law of justice would be established
and spread to the far corners of the earth.

To be fair to Moses, it did prove to be a land flowing with
milk and honey, the law of truth and justice was established and for
the first time in recorded history the world was given a social conscience. The sacredness of the individual, compassion for all mankind
and their fellow creatures, and the clearly declared principle, that the
earth and all that was in it was not man's property, but held only
in trust and therefore to be treated with respect.

This charter of justice formed the basis from which the great religions emerged, and to this day civilized nations have established their legal codes on the principles then enacted. In the course of time various degrees of adaptation and adjustment occurred, and principles that proved to be inconvenient were avoided by those exercising temporal power and authority.

But imperfect people cannot be perfected immediately, it takes a little longer. Although the evolutionary process has been speeded by these precepts, the end product is certainly not yet in sight. Hatred has reigned where love was taught and great wars of destruction were fought in the very name of the Religion that forbade it; one of the most outstanding examples of this was the destruction of the great Christian empire of Byzantia, its fantastic cities and works of art left in ashes, in the wake of hordes that plundered in the name of a Holy Crusade.

All this, of course, did not spring from the failure of the original basic Hebrew teachings but were made possible by the almost frightening versatility of the human mind and its ability to adapt anything which is good in religion, politics or philosophy to serve an evil purpose.

Throughout the long Jewish history in Israel, the Law has always been cherished and mostly observed, but at all times there have been some who have endeavoured to avoid the inconvenient. Usually an honest attempt has been made to live by the standards laid down, probably more so than in any other civilized land.

For twenty-five years now Israel has been in a state of war, and anyone who a few years ago looked over the ramparts at Ramat Rachel outside Jerusalem straight into the barrels of guns at the ready day and night, would have appreciated that there must be some psychological effect on a population existing in such a state of prolonged encirclement. In any other nation so situated for a quarter of a century, the ugliest of human traits would have emerged, but it may be said that to a great degree, the people of Israel have retained their humanity, their compassion, their integrity, and their love of justice. If this be so, then it is undoubtedly due to the inspiration of the past. How long such inspiration can remain under martial conditions is problematical. Slowly but very surely the strain must begin to take effect and under the continued economic and military stress, some aspects begin to develop which are not in conformity with the pristine idealism of Moses.

Western influence too keeps up its unrelenting pressure; the green-eyed gargoyle surveys the scene and voraciously penetrates the land with its materialistic concepts. Happenings now occur which would have been unthinkable twenty-five years ago. The healing art once inspired by divine mercy makes the idea of a doctors' strike repugnant and inconceivable even under a state of economic disadvantage; so long as the shameful practice of flesh-eating persists, the replacement of the abattoirs would be in accordance with the spirit of the Torah, whilst the establishment of a battery system of farming is at complete variance with the prescribed law; even the basic precepts in the Ten Commandments are violated by the failure to grant domestic animals freedom to live a natural life and enjoy the gifts of nature on the Sabbath Day.

Israel was the Promised Land, not a land of promise. Not that prosperity should be shunned. ". . .You shall prosper and help your brother" is a positive command. The fruits of effort shall be used to extend the concept of justice—nowhere is the virtue of poverty commended; but the prophecy of profits and the worship of the wage packet are foreign Gods to which those who love Israel will not bow down. The overwhelming need for the protection of human life must not be confused with the demand for ever-increasing standards of prosperity; contrary to general belief they are not interwoven. Indeed improving the standard of living is a laudable objective, provided always that it does not in itself engender a progressive pollution of the land, sea and air with consequent damage to the health of the people. Provided also that it does not involve the commercialization of sentient animal life with its attendant brutalization of the human mind. Once released these destructive forces cannot be easily restrained, and the chain reaction can eventually destroy a small country.

Israel was promised a garden to tend, not an oil-field to exploit. "I will give the rain of your land in its season, the former rain and the latter rain, that thou mayest gather in thy corn and thy wine and thine oil. And I will give grass in thy field for thy cattle and thou shalt eat and be satisfied." Never has it been indicated that luxury cars and colour televisions will be guaranteed in the land of promise or that the standard of living will be equal to that of the best in Europe or the United States of America. But something far greater would be granted to those who are blessed by living in Israel, the joy of working in a garden and the opportunity to attain spiritual maturity. The question is, will urban sprawl continue and produce a generation of morons, or will it remain a land where the sound of the turtle will be heard and the rose of Sharon will flourish in the valleys? Will it be a land where the sound of silent suffering creatures will echo the cry of Balaam's Ass "What have I done unto thee that thou has smitten me?" or will it be a land dedicated to the glory of creation, where the sounds of the cymbal and the lyre will be heard in the groves and plantations?

However, let it not be inferred from these words, that the dedicated and compassionate people that have given their lives to good government over the years, are unaware of the problems. Neither let us be unmindful of the tremendous efforts that have been made to protect the ecology, the flora and fauna, whilst facing up to the overriding need for the security of the inhabitants. In no other country have such gargantuan achievements been paralleled. Since 1948 each occupant of Israel has absorbed and nurtured two additional refugees. To achieve this, the superhuman efforts made, resulted in Israel having the highest rate of economic growth in the world. Notwithstanding the fact that large numbers of those who arrived at Israel's shores were ill and elderly, the longevity of the people is the second highest in the world; second only to Sweden with its uninterrupted economy and absence of wars for nearly a century.

In the years ahead may peace be at the gates of Israel and may the enemy within be wholly vanquished; a land where each man may sit under the shade of his own fig tree and not be afraid.

May the miracle that is Israel once again shine like a beacon illuminating the true way of life—the interrelationship between man, his Creator, and the earth on which he has been permitted to dwell.

"He sendeth forth springs into the valleys; they run among the mountains. They give drink to every beast of the plain; the wild asses quench their thirst. By them the birds of the heaven have their dwelling, they utter their voice from among the branches. He giveth drink to the mountains from his upper chambers: the earth is satisfied with the fruit of thy works. He causeth grass to grow for the cattle, and herbs for the service of man; that he may bring forth bread from the earth; and wine that maketh glad the heart of man, and oil to make his face to shine, and bread that strengthened man's heart."—PSALM CIV.

A Vegetarian Cookery Book In Yiddish

Perhaps an only copy still exists, after the Churban, of a vegetarian cookery book in Yiddish and published in Vilna, Poland, by the famous house Kletzkin in 1938, the year before the Second World War in which Hitler occupation forces destroyed the millions of Polish Jewry. At that time Jews were still living a fairly normal life. Fania Levando, who was running a Jewish vegetarian restaurant in Vilna, the Kuchnia Dieta-Jarska, compiled and published for Yiddish readers this 235-page volume of vegetarian recipes. These include such Jewish specialties as blintzes, lokshen soup, borsht, kreplach, kugel, cheesecake, tcholent, latkes, kneidlach, shtrudl, tzimmes, fritlach, and honeycake.

In her introduction, "To the Housewives," Fania Levando wrote: "The greatest medical authorities have long ago established that dishes of fruit and vegetables are much healthier and more suited to the human organism than meat dishes. We also know that in our present unhealthy times there is hardly a household without one or more members of the family suffering from some ailment which forbids them to eat meat and makes them keep to a diet. There is also the humanitarian aspect, which finds expression in the vegetarian movement, not to kill any living creature. But we often hear complaints that, 'without meat there is nothing to cook.' "

"So I have decided," Mrs. Levando went on, "to publish this first Yiddish vegetarian cookery book, with over 400 nourishing foods, in order to propagate vegetarian cookery generally, and in particular to serve those housewives who must keep a diet-kitchen."

At the end of her book Fania Levando attaches a number of messages from Yiddish writers and artists who frequented her vegetarian restaurant in Vilna. These include Itzik Manger, J. Giterman, Marc Chagal, Ch. S. Kazdan, Sh. Mendelssohn, N. Buxbaum. Alter Katzisne, who wrote on a menu:

A call to every Semite and Aryan,
From one who is thirty years a vegetarian,
Friends, know that a meal at Levando,
For the vegetarian idea is the best propaganda.

And Abraham Morevski, the famous Russian and Yiddish actor —"I'm an obstinate meat-eater, but I can honestly say that your kneidlach, though innocent of goose-fat, are really first class."

Then the darkness descended.

The Religious Justification For Vegetarianism

Rabbi Joseph Rosenfeld

(Rabbi Rosenfeld was born in the Old City of Jerusalem where his family lived for four generations. For many years Minister of the Sinai Synagogue, Golders Green, London. Adopted vegetarianism for ethical reasons over twenty years ago.)

Those who study the Bible do not need a Rabbi to prove to them that there is religious justification for vegetarianism and those who are ideally convinced of the soundness of the philosophy of vegetarianism as a way of life will continue to practise that ideal whether it is religiously justified or not. Accordingly I have jotted down some biblical and Talmudic references and will be indebted for any sources I fail to quote. And so I had better start, like all things, at the beginning.

All creatures are endowed with two irresistible instincts, self-preservation and procreation and the latter can surely be said to be complementary to the first. When Adam and Eve first roamed the hills and plains that surrounded them they were ignorant of everything, and like all creatures were following their instincts; they did not know how to cohabit or perform all the other functions of life. Each species adopted its own way of life according to its structure and environment; one copied the others and man copied much of his behaviour from them. Unfortunately the baser instincts of animal behaviour have not yet been eradicated from us and become more manifest when these two main instincts are faced with opposition and in danger of remaining unsatisfied. Civilisation has not altered much of our behaviour in our efforts to satisfy these instincts, and later on I will attempt to give you the reasons and humbly suggest the remedy.

For ten generations from Adam to Noah, no flesh of any creature was permitted to be eaten. Gen. 1, 29 is quite explicit. "Behold I have given you every herb yielding seed which is upon the face of all the earth, and every tree, in which is the fruit of the tree yielding seed — to you it shall be for food." And not only was the instruction directed to man but also to all creatures as stated in verse 30. "And to every beast of the earth, and to every fowl of the air, and to every thing that creepeth upon the earth, wherein there is a living soul, I have given every green herb for food. And it was so." It is on these verses that Rabbi Judah bases his statements in Tractate Sanehdrin 59, 2. Up to Noah the eating of flesh was prohibited.

At this stage I should like to pass before you a problem and I cannot trace that it has been raised by any of the known and renowned commentators.

Everyone knows the story of Cain and Abel, as related in Genesis, chapter 4, but it would be instructive to review it in order to show what is so puzzling about the sequence of events. Cain devoted himself to tilling the ground and the produce of the land while Abel became a shepherd of sheep. Cain brought an offering to God of the fruit of the land, apparently not of the best and God did not show favour. Abel brought his offering from the fullest and choicest of his sheep to which God showed favour. Cain was angry and God told him if he would do better he would be forgiven. Then Cain said something to Abel and when they were in the field Cain arose and killed his brother Abel.

There are several questions which present themselves to us. What was wrong with Cain's offering? True it was not of the choicest of the fruit, still it was an offering and after all it was he who first thought of the idea of a thanks-offering. So why was he slighted? The second question is what was it that Cain said to Abel before he killed him? The Bible does not tell us. The third and more potent question is why was Cain not sentenced to death for the capital crime he committed? His only punishment was banishment from society and what is more puzzling, is Cain's plea, "Is then my sin too great to be forgiven? Anyone who will find me will kill me." God presented him with a sign to save him from being assassinated. An amazing plea from the lips of a murderer and an even more surprising response from the judge of all things on earth. Seven generations later, Cain's great-great-grandson was out hunting and as his sight was failing him, his boy accompanied him to pin-point the position of any animal. Cain was mistaken for an animal and was killed by Lemech. On discovering his mistake, Lemech clapped his hands in remorse and killed his own son in the process. These questions troubled me very much and I failed to find the answers until a little while ago when another very curious question came to my mind. The question which perplexed me was why Abel was killed and I had an irresistible desire to delve deeper until I found a satisfactory explanation.

We know that no one was punished unless something had been done to deserve it, especially when it concerned capital offence. Now what did Abel do to deserve death? Nowhere in the Bible or anywhere else is there any hint that he sinned against the Lord or man, certainly not to deserve death. Then why was he murdered? The answer came like a flash and I realised that this would answer the other questions. For ten generations up to Noah no creature was allowed to eat flesh. No living creature was to be killed by either man or beast for any purpose whatsoever. Although this purpose for which Abel killed the fattest and choicest of his sheep was an offering to God it did not alter the fact that he shed the blood of an innocent sheep, albeit for a selfless motive. The answer to my first question as to why Cain's offering was not accepted is simple. Here is the first lesson of how to shape our characters. When we make an offering it should be of the best. God accepted Abel's offering rather than Cain's not because the one was of a living creature and the other was of the fruit of the land.

Does then the Lord require animal sacrifices? Isaiah 1, 11: "To what purpose is the multitude of your sacrifices unto me" said the Lord. "I am full of the burnt-offerings of rams and the fat of the fed beasts and I delight not in the blood of bullocks or of the lambs or he-goats," and 22, 13: "And behold joy and gladness, slaying oxen and killing sheep, eating flesh and drinking wine—let us eat and drink for tomorrow we shall die." "Surely this iniquity shall not be expiated by you till ye die."

We can now understand what Cain said to Abel before he killed him. "Why did you slay those innocent lambs? If you desired to bring a thank-offering to the Lord then you should have brought him from the toil of your hands and not at the expense of the lives of others." This also explains why Cain was not sentenced to die immediately but was postponed for seven generations. Cain, and this is my own personal opinion, thought that in killing his brother he was carrying out the commandment of the Lord. Did not God say, Genesis 9, 5: "But the blood of your souls I will demand. I will demand it from the hand of every beast and from the hand of man. . . ."

I am no longer puzzled and perplexed why Abel died. He was the first to break the law of God. Cain was not the first man to kill, it was Abel who first shed the blood and took the life of a living creature and so had to die in consequence of his deed. There is no difference between depriving the life and soul of man and that of an animal. Does not King Solomon tell us Eccl. 3, 21: "Who knows the spirit of the sons of man ascends above, and the spirit of the cattle descends down into the earth."

In my contact with many vegetarians I detect that the greater majority have forsaken a carnivorous diet for health reasons rather than for the lofty ideal itself that it is wrong in principle to be carnivorous. It is, of course, right and proper that we should look after our health and adhere to a diet which preserves and prolongs life which surely a vegetarian diet does. But if you reduce the ethical values of vegetarianism to the pursuit of health then you are just as likely to revert to your former habits of flesh eating when someone will cite the example of a number of people who live to the age of ninety and even to one-hundred and who have been eating flesh all their lives. To think of vegetarianism in terms of health only is equating our lives with that of the animal. I have always wondered what Solomon, the cleverest of all men, meant when he said, Ecc. 3, 19: "And the pre-eminence of man over beast is nought for all is vanity." Surely man and especially men like Solomon himself could not be said that they are not of greater eminence than the animal. It is inconceivable that man with all his apparent superiority, thought, design and deeds, could be classified on the same level as the beast. Yet this is what Solomon seems to tell us. On reflection however, I came to the conclusion, and incidently this is my own opinion, that the translators have all erred in their interpretation of the last part of this verse. The mistake lies in the translation of the word *Kee*; this word has several meanings and in this context the only sensible and correct translation would be *when*. The whole verse assumes now quite a different aspect and meaning thus: "and the pre-eminence of man over beast is naught when all is vanity."

If man is occupied throughout his life in the pursuit of his basic instincts, eating, drinking and the seeking of pleasures, in this sense there is no advantage of man over beast. The animal likewise is preoccupied all its life in the pursuit of satisfying its basic instincts. It too has its pleasures, limited though they may be; the coolness of water, the shade of a tree, the warmth of the sun. This is why I am not impressed with vegetarians who are concerned only with their state of health. Far better to adopt a vegetarian way of life as an ideal, only then will you be a good and convincing example to others.

Admittedly it is difficult for Jewish people to discard their carnivorous way of life; to provide for Sabbaths and festivals the expensive delicacies of meat and fish. But the Talmud (Pessachim 109a) states "Rabbi Yehuda who said that there is no Simcha only with meat, agrees that this only applied at the time when the Temple was in existence." We also find in Tracte Babba Bathra 608, Rabbi Yishmael said "from the day that the Holy Temple was destroyed it would have been right to have imposed on ourselves the law prohibiting the eating of flesh." But the Rabbis have laid down a wise and logical ruling that the authorities must not impose any decree unless the majority of the members of the Community are able to abide by it. Otherwise the law and those who administer it get into disrepute."

That is why ten generations after Adam man was so corrupt that, like the ferocious animal, he would tear a limb from a living creature, eat it and drink its blood. The Torah, realising that it would take many generations of special training before man's soul would become completely refined, permitted the eating of flesh after Noah but with many reservations and restrictions. Hence the humane laws of Shechita and the dietary laws of Kasruth. The soaking for an hour or half an hour and salting of Kosher meat before we are allowed to cook it, in order to extract the maximum amount of blood of which we are not allowed to partake. "For blood is the soul." Life, thought, character, behaviour, are all contained in the chemicals comprised in the blood. The less of the animal blood in man, the purer his soul becomes, the nearer he gets to the Divine being. When the Israelites were near the Mishcon, the Sanctuary, the eating of flesh was forbidden to them (Orlah 2, Misnah 17). It is true, therefore, that the eating of flesh is looked upon as a lust and Jewish law aims to restrict and arrest that diet. Thousands of years of adhering to these traditional dietary laws have resulted in a gradual process of purification to the soul and there is no doubt that these teachings had a profound effect upon the civilised nature of the Jew who as a rule is rarely found guilty of wanton cruelty, either to animals or man. The best story I have heard which illustrates this lack of cruelty for the sake of sport or revenge is the following: Yankel and Mendel were in the habit of discussing aspects of the law every morning after the service at the Synagogue. One morning they became involved in a very heated argument when Yankel called Mendel a swindler. The latter was enraged and he told Yankel that the only way to settle the matter was by duel with guns. It was accordingly arranged to meet the next morning at 6 A.M. in the local park. Mendel and his seconds arrived punctually at six o'clock and it was nearing seven and Yankel had still not arrived. Mendel was about to depart calling his opponent a coward, when he saw Yankel's second running towards him. They came to apologise on behalf of Yankel who forgot that he had Yahrzeit (Memorial Service) and could not come before eight o'clock but in the meantime he had no objection if Mendel started shooting in the meanwhile. These estimable characteristics of mercy, kindness, compassion, and charitableness so much pronounced among the Jewish people is a result of following for generations the laws of the Torah and the instructions of the Prophets. David said in Psalm 145, 9: "God is good to all and his tender mercies are over all His works." Force of habit leads us to think that we cannot or must not do without flesh, but the Torah does not say you must or should eat flesh. Knowing the weakness of man it permitted only certain animals and then only after Shechita had been performed which was the humane way of ending the life of a creature. But we must train ourselves to discard that habit which has been ingrained in us for generations. Every creature has a right to live and no one has a right to destroy life.

(Isaiah 66, 3): He that killeth an ox is as he that slayeth a man." As long as man is ready to slay an animal to satisfy his needs or his pleasures, he will be ready to kill his fellow man for similar reasons. Isaiah's vision which is so simply yet so forcefully expressed in chapter 11, 6, can only come about if his prophecy in the verses which follow (7-9) come true. And the wolf shall dwell with the lamb and the leopard shall lie down with the kid, and the calf and the young lion and the fatling together and a little child shall lead them." (Verses 7-9): And the cow and the bear shall feed; their young ones shall lie down together; and the lion shall eat straw like the ox. They shall not hurt nor destroy in all my holy mountain for the earth shall be full of the knowledge of the Lord as the waters cover the sea.

Tell Him All This

Extract from An Address by Peter Roberts, N.D.A., C.D.A.
Administrator of 'Compassion in World Farming'

"Eat up your meat, Jimmy; it will make you big and strong"
and, "Eat up what the Good Lord gave you."

If we are to believe Darwin's Theory of Evolution, we were
descended from the vegetarian ape and about three-quarters of a
million years ago turned away from the vegetarian culture to one of
carnivorism, perhaps under the influence of the Ice Age. In addition
to the vegetarian origin of the human race, it is evident that there are
still more vegetarians in the world than meat eaters—which may
suggest that it is the latter who are the nonconforming cranks, not
us!

Three-quarters of a million years may not be long in the world's
evolution, and we could go for another such period as carnivores
were it not for one factor—Technology. Its effect on us may be seen
in the loss of amenities, in pollution, world hunger, disease and maybe
war. Either we must change, or God may politely ask Man to leave the
planet.

We must take a new image and break out of the self-imposed
wall that we tend to build around ourselves. It is no longer good
enough to be circulating leaflets and lecturing within the walls. We
have to go outside and persuade people there to confront their
children with the truth and stop insulting them with, "Eat up your
meat, it is good for you."

Sonny must not be told that the meat in front of him the Good Lord gave. He must be told rather that it is the muscle from the leg of a calf, that the calf was conceived artificially, denied its mother's love, reared in a dark box, and fed on an unnatural diet; that it was transported across one or more countries in terror and probably slaughtered in pain; that it never smelled the wind or saw a tree or laid on the grass.

Tell him all that without emotion so that he can make his own unemotional judgement. . . .

Do not tell him that his meat will make him strong: tell him rather that the drug residues in the meat may cripple him. Tell him that he can only have his veal on the condition that his Hindu brother on the other side of the world starves.

Tell him all this and stop the pretence.

All the resources, research and know-how at present squandered on the feeding of animals can be diverted to the feeding of humans who are at present starving and ignored. . . .Technology has got us into this mess — it can also get us out.

Where technology is applied to the production of food, there should be no animal involved. Plant materials can be processed as easily as through animals and a lot better.

For the countryside, the old techniques were better than the modern, and were more scientifically sound. Nature allowed the alternation of exhausting and recuperative crops and also controlled weeds, pests, and plant disease without the need for toxic chemicals. The countryside was also a place where children could have fun, unconsciously orientating themselves to Nature; the farm-worker could have pride in his work.

Suddenly buildings emerge in the countryside, not production units but processing units needing vast inputs. Protein, usually from hungry nations that could themselves do with it, barley in astronomic tonnage achieved by continuing corn production. In place of the quiet skills there is now the mad headlong rush to harvest the grain and burn the straw so as to make way as quickly as possible for the next crop. This can cause plant diseases and the breakdown in the structure of the soil — deserts in the making!

Pollution is another factor. The old cyclic return of wastes in the biologic economy is gone and the closed cycle is now a straight line with big inputs of toxic chemicals and equally big outputs of pollutants. Over the past twenty years fertiliser usage has risen five-fold compared with the grain yield.

There is also the cruelty issue. Battery chickens for egg production, broilers which will end up as oven-ready chickens, calves in veal units, pigs in cages (in iron frames to prevent them lying on their litters), lambs in cages, mass-bred by hormone treatment of the ewes. Some are in slum conditions, others more clinical, but to the bird or animal they are doubtlessly very alike in confinement, monotony, and stress. The unnatural lighting, inadequate water supply, lack of attention to the removal of dung, overcrowding, difficulty in feeding, feather picking, disease, and the daily toll of dead creatures introduces the threat to human health.

Some say that plant protein is inferior and that meat protein is necessary for health. The opposite is the case. The Central Food Technology Institute of Madras has proved this with its introduction of Indian Multi-purpose Meal (oilseed protein and cheap cereal) in famine areas, saving many children from the dreaded Kwashiorker, the famine disease.

The final success is the acceptance by the American Food and Drug Administration of textured vegetable protein food for use in American schools and the U.S. child feeding programme. Official approval implies that with T.V.P. the American child will get all that he or she is used to obtaining from meat. Tell him *All* This!

I Was An "M.D."

(Muscular Dystrophy)

(Peter Clifford, the vegetarian champion cyclist, writer and folksinger, and how he conquered Muscular Dystrophy)

D-Day means very little to those of you who have not passed your first quarter century, but those who have and can recall "The Great Divide" will understand what I mean when I tell you I am in my third lease of life and mean to make the most of it.

My nickname during D-Day rehearsals was "Salt-Peter." I was attached to a Canadian Division and found myself in a specially trained outfit working behind enemy lines on special service. The mischief we caused came to an abrupt halt, however, and I was dragged out of a tight corner with a stomach injury, survived after three operations and left France loaded with penicillin.

It took the best part of twelve months to pull through and by the mercy of God I made it and began a new life in the fields of research which would create instead of destroy. Things went along with great promise until my second D-Day when I landed in hospital and was counted among the 200 polio victims.

The year 1950 was particularly bad for this illness and at first the condition could not be treated at all. Patients died every day and I was the last of that first group and the only one to survive. Newspapers are not always allowed to tell the story at the time (professional ethics?) and today, nearly twenty years later, there is plenty of evidence that the vaccines used in the later stages to fight the plague were valueless. First, the Salk vaccine proved quite false, killing far more than those who really did have polio. Now it can be told that none of these have proved successful and instead of poliomyelitis we have a multiplicity of my-op-ath-ies (diseases of the muscles) and those polio cases which came through have been put into different groups. Mine was first called Myopathy, then Myositis, then Muscular Dystrophy. There are some 30,000 known cases and this figure is fluctuating because it is a killer disease. A certain "gonna" if it is discovered in childhood and a miserable progressive wasting of the limbs until an age limit of twenty or thirty. Complete incapacitation for older and "milder" cases. Medical science is up against the wall, shocking, but true.

In March this year I drew the attention of my own plight to a Professor who had come down from the North of England for an M.D. Symposium. He made a brief examination of me and decided that though incredible, there was no doubt in his mind that I had M.D. I told him that whilst other patients had wasted away reading blood and thunder paperbacks from the Red Cross trolley, I had secretly begun to study medicine in their own hospital libraries and after tracing the condition to the inability of the genes to metabolise and utilise Pottassium-Chloride, I began a more thorough effort to have my diet reformed. This gamble against drugs and beaurocracy paid off. Those who did not believe me including the very consultant (Lord Brain) who gave me up, ("you have about three years to live and less if you go on with these stupid contradictions") have passed away.

First, one must believe in oneself, then learn that we do not deceive nature, we only deceive ourselves. My weight at one time was seven stone at five feet six inches and I had a very weak abdomen wall. I needed much more than artificial aids. The physiotherapy I felt was too mild and the dieticians obstinate and rarely communicative or progressive enough to help me with my ideas, so after four years of hospitalisation I escaped. Finding some "digs" nearby, I made myself an outpatient and finally it was the encouragement from a man twice my age who was a vegetarian and already well-known in Europe, as a great stayer on a bicycle, who came to my rescue. Rene Menzies, in his broken English said to me, "Sit on this saddle and pedal low gears as I do and you will get better, you may even walk again. Everything else you are doing seems to be just right." His boss, Louis Cammillous (Cyclo Gears) gave me a bike with a thirty-four-inch gear, pretty low but oh what a pleasure. Although I always have a hard winter (don't we all) I can ride, walk and even run; who knows with care I will reach one-hundred years of age. Most people do of course but it only takes them fifty years to do it.

My cycle became a mobile walking stick and we traveled many miles together in peace and solitude. Club life flourished and in the summer I was racing secretary to the Three Spires and had formed two other clubs. During the winter months, social work with the Coventry Cycling Club and singing with local bands kept me busy. It was one of those crazy moments deciding to go for the record to London and back, that started the next phase and I began to build up my shape for greater all-round body efficiency. My own ideas blended into physical and nutritional therapy and the 180-mile ride took nine hours, three minutes. Even then, as I made the turn in London I knew I had to return; I hadn't got a cat and had never heard the Bow Bells but, like Whittington I came and never looked back. Here I threw off my leg callipers for good and all that remains of my aids are a pair of crutches nailed to the wall by my bed as one would cross a pair of swords. It is a symbol of defiance.

To start training again was my first and greatest need; food I could do without but exercise never. I met Lou Ravelle and it was then I began an almost nonstop seven-day week, three-year plan of teaching, free training, and specialisation in a culture which grew roots and made me many friends.

Later I owned two gyms, the second was a much more modern health centre which boasted a health bar and a library with some very excellent help at times. Some people scorn physical culture work but it is usually the defeated and undernourished who do so. Newspapers and writers think that a little "snigger" sells more copies than any sincere reporting, and this of course is true of all minor activities. Even vegetarians and cyclists have to accept ill-informed writing, so we provide ourselves with our own specialised magazines.

Like those wonderful examples of manpower, John Grimek and George Eiffermann, I have taken rather more kindly to writing than

I would have thought possible. My first work was a book about the history of the *Tour de France*, the world's greatest cycle race which began in 1903 and the publishers, Stanley Paul, want a revised edition. We have a book on the *Tour of Britain* profusely illustrated with 100 photographs and diagrams and a yearbook on cycling (the first in Britain for one-hundred years) called *On the Stocks* and another which has been in print for five years I have called *Fatigue Barrier* which is what all this is about.

We all learn by our mistakes but do we ever really put those mistakes right? Why do we sleep so much, eat so often, spend so much on entertainment? What would we really do again if we had a second chance? All these questions we have asked ourselves time and time again and do nothing about our own basically definable *Fatigue Barrier*. The passion and will to go on and conquer new fields is often lost in the battle with our digestive systems at the meal table. That lack of predetermination, is that it? When people tell me something is impossible I like to remind them that nothing is impossible, only for those who do nothing.

To those who say that cycling is too much like hard work I would say that one can only become a good cyclist by doing the hard work of learning how and then it becomes easier every day. Cycling is mechanical walking, it is five times faster and you can travel five times further with the same effort. I even knew a fellow who once couldn't walk but used to go hell for leather on a bike and still does—it's me!

The Vision Of Vegetarianism And Peace

(BOOK OF JOB)

(Rabbi Kook, the first Chief Rabbi of Israel, was a vegetarian from the age of 10 years. His good works and profound religious studies endeared him, not only to all sections of the population in Israel, but to Jews all over the world.)

Translation by A. Tzimchony

There is one fundamental branch of the virtues we have inherited from our forefathers which is the very highest. This is where the community stands in accordance with the convictions on which it leans.

There is also the belief in a sweet dream of those more extreme idealists with their instinct and just humane sentiment to examine the judgment on behalf of the living creatures with deep understanding.

Most of the cruel philosophies went further and further in their outlook on human ethics, from the general philosophical point of view already shared (or held) by man. Those philosophies, each in their own way, tried to strangle or to supress completely the righteous feeling for animal life. In fact they have not and will not, with all their lecturings and preachings, suppress the right moral inborn habit which the Creator of man has planted into him. We belong to the animal world and therefore (through those philosophies) our righteous feelings and inborn habits become like a burning coal which gets weaker and dimmer and eventually is buried under mountains of earth and ashes. Nevertheless it is still impossible for them to deny the sentiments in every feeling heart. The great loss of general ethics and the suppression of good noble moral feelings, not to take life to satisfy one's own needs or pleasures, is a failure of the human race which must not survive.

Our Rabbis (the memory of the righteous be blessed) it appears, did not go into these studies and philosophies, but they tell us about the holy Rabbi (Yehudi the Prince) who was punished with great physical sufferings for exclaiming to a calf who was being dragged to the slaughterhouse (and sought his protection), "Don't hold on to the hem of my coat, you have been created for this purpose." He was cured from his sufferings, so the story tells us, through showing compassion to vermin. In this instance they did not act as other philosophers who make light into darkness, but sought to clarify their opinion through this story, because it is impossible to imagine the Lord of all deeds with compassion on all life, should make an eternal law such as this: namely, that it is not possible for the human race to survive if they trespass this moral sentiment and kill.

Let the commandment "Thou shalt not kill" be understood to include all living creatures.

The scholar and the thinker should have no doubt that the domination mentioned in the Torah "and have dominion over the fish of the sea, and over the fowl of the air, and over every living thing that moveth upon the earth"[1] does not refer to the domination of a tyrant, tormenting his people and his slaves, only to satisfy his private needs and desires. God forbid that such an ugly law of slavery should be sealed eternally in the world of God "Who is good to all and whose tender mercies are over all His works"[2]. Who said "The world is built upon mercy."[3] This is clearly indicated since, according to the interpretations of our sages of those sentences of the Bible which prove that Adam did not have meat as a food. "Behold I have given you

every herb bearing seed, . . .and every tree, in which is the fruit
of the tree yielding seed; to you it shall be for meat".[4] Only when
the sons of Noah came after the flood, He allowed them flesh.
". . .even as the green herb have I given you all things."[5] Is it
possible to imagine after this that a moral benefit of great value,
which has already been in fact a possession of mankind should be
lost forever. About this and similar problems it is said "I shall think
back to the remote past and I shall grant justice to My creations."[6]
Enlightenment in the future will widen our resources and free us
from this problem.

1. Genesis 1: 28.
2. Psalm 145: 9.
3. Psalm 89: 2.
4. Genesis 2:29.
5. Genesis 9: 3.
6. Job 36: 3.

Mother Earth

(EDITORIAL)

"If knowledge be the mark, to know thee shall suffice;
Well learned is that tongue that will ever thee commend;
All ignorant that soul that sees thee without wonder. . .
Thine eye Jove's lightning bears, thy voice is dreadful thunder."
(Shakespeare)

To see without wonder—to plunder without thought—to ravage without pity. Perforce Mother Earth brings forth her great family, and with love provides their needs in abundance and with infinite variety. With deep satisfaction they suckle at her ample bosom and draw strength and character from her ever-flowing fount of beauty; they delve deeply into the horn of plenty and gather rare gifts of scented delight. They derive inspiration and invention from her ever-changing moods, and in the security of her constancy, embark upon adventure that affects generations as yet unborn.

"A mother can support many children—but many children cannot support one mother." Like many folk sayings, this adage portrays clearly the frailty of human nature and gently brings to mind man's ingratitude and forgetfulness of benefits enjoyed. Ungrateful indeed are the firstborn of Mother Earth; they forage without restraint and destroy without feeling; her verdant beauty is scarred without reason; with ruthlessness her strength is sapped by forcing from her untimely sustenance; her forests are razed that newsprint might spread the

message of greed and lust, and thus by baseless rumour sow the seeds of dissent between brother and brother. With unrelenting sadism they encompass and destroy her younger offspring and celebrate festivities in great charnel-houses where they consume the charred remains; they place a lifeless body on the Sabbath table to rejoice in its creation.

"*. . .That thou mayest gather in thy corn and thy wine and thine oil. . .and thou shalt eat and be satisfied.*" But they are not satisfied — they wait not for Mother Earth to give forth her produce, it shall be dragged from her without consent — it shall be taken by caesarean operation. Her fruits shall not suffice; foul delicacies alone shall satiate the depraved palates; severed tongues and song birds grilled on charcoal, stuffed throats of birds and pheasants soaked in wine; no limits shall be set and no compassion can ever arise from the faetid stomach of the destroyer. Not even the restraint of impaired health shall stay the knife or awaken the conscience of the self-seeker.

A beautiful garden vibrant with the music of myriad life forms is provided but they prefer to dwell in the precincts of the slaughter-houses.

They feed on imprisoned battery creatures and foul the sweet rain with death-dealing chemicals; they poison their own beings and confine themselves in battery dwellings, they make pilgrimages to the Hiltons the Waldorfs and the Grosvenors, where they offer sacrifices to the glorification of themselves; they are a generation that knows not the biblical injunction to bring forth bread from Mother Earth with the sweat of the brow.

Days were when Adam delved and Eve span but today each is a gentleman; or at least is so garbed with all the trappings that go therewith and none of the substances. But the quality of mercy has not ceased entirely, many arise with true feeling and understanding; some call themselves Friends of the Earth — they plant trees in busy fume-filled streets and protest by the polluted streams.

Not in logic or by the study of mathematics shall relief be found; nor by formal meetings where deep and selfish motives cause partici-pants to utter pretentious platitudes. And plenopotentiaries discuss the Ecology, not as a labour of love walking on foot to the meeting place, but as commercial representatives driving in oversize limousines which bring further pollution both to the air and to the sincerity of their endeavours.

Only by tenderness of heart shall Mother Earth be consoled — in the storms her tears are borne, in the mighty thunder her cries of agony are heard, and in her eruptions flow the lava of her festering wounds as she writhes in the suffering that her firstborn has brought upon her. Those who are her friends will protect her, care for her little ones, guard her beauty, provide for her future well-being and pray for her welfare; so that with love and devotion her great family shall live in peace and she will bestow a blessing of health on all that dwell with her.

In her realm are numerous spheres of love and hate, of fear and joy, which we can neither see nor hear nor comprehend. To which of these invisible dimensions shall we add our contribution?

The Silly Season
EDITORIAL

The Jewish calendar must surely be unique in its planned frustration of a gregarious people bent upon celebrating any and every possible event.

In early spring preparations for Passover commence avidly, followed by the "Sefira" period lasting several weeks; by this time the school holiday season casts its lengthy shadow whilst almost everyone peregrinates to and fro. No sooner has the last family arrived home tired and in need of a rest, than the High Festivals are upon us, New Year, Day of Atonement, and Succot! By this time it is well into October, fortitude and patience are wilting, until finally frustration is released with an unbroken and remorseless round of weddings, Barmitzvahs, charity dinners, and what have you. Everyone invites everyone else and in the panic of clashing dates and plates, the catering fraternity struggle on with a stoic persistence and relentlessness worthy of an honoured place in history.

Profusion produces conformity, perhaps even monotony, but perpetual motion demands that an invitation begets an invitation and the circle ever widens.

Shall we not stop for a brief moment, take a deep breath and consider whether in this head-long rush of sociability perhaps one or two ethics are being trampled underfoot?

Most of these occasions are to commemorate joyous and creative events in the lives of the celebrants which often have a deep religious significance. To what extent is consideration given to this aspect? For example, does a host ever consider whether perhaps there may be cruelty and sacrilege involved in the choice of a menu? For example when portions of fowl are passed around, has anyone given a thought that these birds once breathed with us the same breath of life?

"Giver of life to every living thing!
Beasts of the field, and birds that heavenward wing. . ."

Throughout their lives incarcerated in battery cages nine inches square, suffering and frustrated they fight — and suffer the penalty of having their breaks removed. Gone, their natural right to move around and thus easy prey to disease: pumped full of dangerous antibiotics they succumb to degenerative diseases so much so that Ministry figures show that one in every three suffers from cancerous growths.

And what of the young calves, highly developed sentient creatures, reared in darkened cells for three or six months, never to see the light of day, or to frolic in the Spring grass; condemned to stand on slats until the day of their death, chained so that they may not lie down to rest, fed on iron-deficient diet to produce anaemia and white flesh for the carnivore's greater delight! Is it really celebration to remove the stilled tongue, to chop and and spice the enlarged, diseased, fatty, degenerated liver of this tortured and drugged animal? Are not these transgressions against our Jewish teachings of compassion and shall they be considered lightly at religious celebrations?

When the smell of burning flesh pervades the corridors of the charnel-houses and the guests are assembled for the macabre feast, shall no-one conceive the vision of the slaughterer, bespattered with blood, taking the life from the crying imploring creature? Shall not the jovial expansive feelings of those assembled have a thought for grisly activities that preceded the preparation of that upon which they are about to feed? Does not the ancient love of freedom, justice, and kindliness reach back even unto lesser creatures? "To man and to all creatures have I given a living soul." Shall not the Barmitzvah boy in his proud emergence to manhood be guided by gentleness and consideration, not only for his fellow men but also for his fellow creatures who have been incarcerated and forcibly taken to the slaughter?

It is not callousness that perpetuates this cruelty, only thoughtlessness, but ignorance is not innocence, and the celebrants, every one, carry the burden of this suffering and pay the penalty to be exacted.

What then is the alternative?

Should not our celebrants know that from the kindly produce of the earth, sumptious banquets may be prepared, delightful to the eye and delicious to the tongue, surpassing the wildest demands of the gourmet, as costly as the occasion demands and appreciated by the most hardened socialite?

Let all who wish their Simcha to be blessed with the sanctity of life; who have the imagination and good taste to entertain their guests in a delightful and original manner, retire from the chicken and salmon race and convert these animal crematoriums into halls of rejoicing where "all creatures shall praise the Lord."

Many public figures, as guests, attend these Simchas with unfailing regularity and eat much of the emaciated and hormone-injected viands. Is it hospitality to further encourage among them thrombosis, ulcers, liver, kidney, and many other diseases?

The Borgias poisoned selected guests for a purpose.

Our celebrants poison all their guests indiscriminately without purpose.

Silly Season indeed!